Modern Ivory Carving

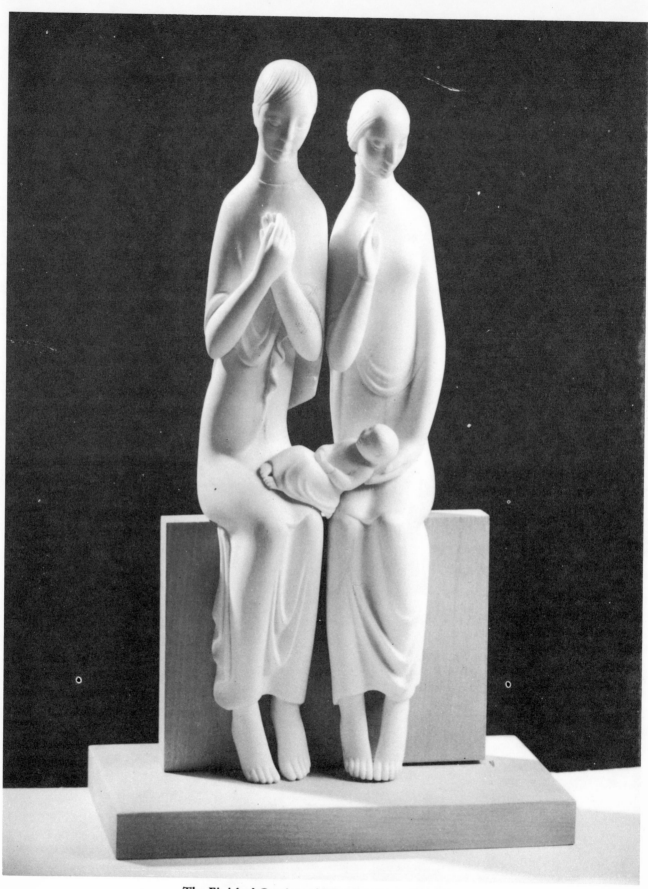

The Finished Carving of "Family Group." Notice
how the baby has changed position slightly from
the sketch model on page 17. (Owned by Thomas
M. Drake)

Modern Ivory Carving

Carson I. A. Ritchie

South Brunswick and New York: A. S. Barnes and Company
London: Thomas Yoseloff Ltd

A. S. Barnes and Co., Inc.
Cranbury, New Jersey 08512

Thomas Yoseloff Ltd
108 New Bond Street
London W1Y OQX, England

Library of Congress Cataloging in Publication Data

Ritchie, Carson I A
  Modern ivory carving.

  1. Ivory carving—History. I. Title.
NK5890.R5   1972   736.6   75-146773
ISBN 0-498-07785-3

Also by the Author

Ivory Carving
Carving Shells and Cameos

Printed in the United States of America

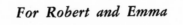

For Robert and Emma

Contents

Acknowledgments

I should like to thank Her Majesty The Queen for her gracious permission to use photographs of the Duke of Clarence's tomb at Windsor.

The museums, art galleries, and libraries that helped me in my research for this book are too numerous to mention individually. I should, however, like to record my gratitude to: L. M. Forbes of the Library, the Polar Research Institute, Cambridge, England; Lloyd's Register of Shipping, London; Comrade A. Runkov of the Trade Delegation of The USSR in The United Kingdom; M. Luwel of the *Musée Royal De L'Afrique Centrale,* Tervuren, Belgium; Charles Avery and A. F. Radcliffe of the Victoria and Albert Museum, London; Herr Stockner, *Oberstudiendirektor* of the *Fachschule Für Holz Und Elfenbein,* Erbach, West Germany; Miss Rina Prentice of the National Maritime Museum, Greenwich, England; Miss Christa Merkes of the *Deutches Kulturinstitut,* London; Professor Lockhart of the Anthropological Museum, Aberdeen, Scotland; James Boyd, Director of the Museums and Art Galleries, Dundee, Scotland; Miss Dale Idiens of the Royal Scottish Museum, Edinburgh, Scotland; M. Pierre Bazin of the *Musée de Dieppe,* Seine Inferieure, France; M. Pierre Georgel, *Chargé de mission à l'Ambassade de France,* London; Mlle. F. van Haelewyck, *Attachée Culturelle* of the *Ambassade De Belgique,* London; Philip Chadwick Smith, Curator of Maritime History at the Peabody Museum, Boston, Massachusetts; Douglas Matthews of the London Library, London; M. Laisne, the Dieppe Librarian; and W. A. Southern and John Bartlett of Hull Museum, England.

Many sculptors, and their relatives, helped me by either providing information or by lending me photographs and sculptures (which were usually family treasures as well as art treasures). They include Gwynneth Holt, Jeanne Bell, M. Joyce Bidder, Mrs. Marjorie Gray, M. Colette, Captains C. E. Parkes and Spencer Johnson, contemporary experts on scrimshaw, Dunstan Pruden, Donald Potter, the late Alan Durst, Robert Robertson, and many others.

I should like to single out in particular Dr. Hans Werner Hegemann, Director of the *Erbacher Elfenbeinmuseum,* Erbach, Odenwald, West Germany, without whose "Elfenbein" it would be impossible to understand modern German ivory carving; Commander George Naish, the Director of the Royal National Maritime Museum, Greenwich, England, to whom I fear I must have proved something of an Ancient Mariner; Mrs. Ginsberg of the Victoria and Albert Museum, London, who explained to me how Victorian corsets worked; Mr. E. R. Beecher, also of the Victoria and Albert, who initiated me into the mysteries of caring for ivories; and Messrs. Friedlein of the Natural Products, Kudu House, The Minories, London, E.C.3., for lending me scrimshaw and putting their generations'-old experience of selling ivory at my disposal.

Mr. and Mrs. Handley-Read were kindness

itself in answering my many queries about Victorian sculpture.

Mrs. Eva Light and Mrs. Ursula Williams skillfully piloted me through the shoals of the German language. I owe them both particular thanks.

Introduction: Visit to an Ivory Carver's Studio

There can be no better way of introducing the history of ivory carving than by watching an ivory carver of today at work in her studio. Ivory carving has changed less over the past 200 years than any other kind of art. Although there may seem to be no connection between Gwynneth Holt, Britain's foremost ivory sculptor, and all the other ivory carvers whose work is going to be described in this book (a rather mixed assortment that includes Yankee whalers in the South Pacific making scrimshaw, British whalers laboring at the same task among icebergs in the Arctic, German counts making chessmen as a dilettante hobby, Russians carving superb vases as presents for foreign potentates, Yakut nomads making ivory models for magical purposes, French carvers at work for princesses visiting the Normandy seaside, an English knight making ivory figures for the tomb of Queen Victoria's favorite grandson, and American prisoners of war making ivory ships in the dungeons of British castles), I can assure the reader that ivory carvers are all a lot nearer to one another than might at first appear. To take just one instance, the tools that Miss Holt uses, and that can be seen in the illustration lying on her work table, were given to her by Richard Garbe, a famous English ivory sculptor. He was born, in 1876, into a family of ivory and tortoiseshell workers, whose working methods probably went back to at least the year 1800, when this survey of modern ivory carving begins.

A visit to a carver at work may also help the reader to evaluate some of the statements that he may have heard about ivory sculpture in the past, statements that are often put forward rather naïvely by art historians, such as the assertion that ivory is very soft when it is fresh, but once it is allowed to season, it becomes harder than stone; that it can be polished just by wiping over with a rag; and so forth.

The Sculptor at work—Gwynneth Holt carving. Notice how one hand acts as a break on the other and prevents too much ivory being chiseled off with one stroke.

Gwynneth Holt's Studio. Note Richard Garbe's
ivory carving tools lying on the bench and the
flower piece sketched on a block of ivory in the
foreground.

So far as I know, nobody has ever bothered
to describe how an ivory carver sets about his
task, yet very few people ever get an opportunity
to watch one at work, and there is no art without the artist.

Gwynneth Holt lives in a tiny village called
Broomfield, in Essex, which, like so many parts
of East Anglia, looks a little like New England.
Many Essex Puritans fled to America in the 17th
century. The clapboard houses they built there
closely resemble those of that era still standing
in Broomfield. I had walked past plenty of clapboard houses, right round the Village Green in
fact, before I found someone who could direct

me to Miss Holt's house, which, appropriately
enough for a famous Catholic sculptor, is not a
17th-century Puritan style house, but a pre-
reformation Tudor cottage that used to be part
of a monastery estate. The village sexton, who
had volunteered to be my guide, left his grass
cutting in the churchyard and trudged along be-
side me through the narrow streets of the village.
He knew Miss Holt's house well. It was only
the other day that he had cut down a cedar in
the churchyard garth and taken her some of the
wood for carving. He had seen her sculptures
for the first time, he told me, and been very impressed by them. Ivory carving is one of the few

modern arts that does not frighten or bemuse the man in the street, as opposed to the professed connoisseur. Perhaps this is because an ivory statue is so small that you can usually get on friendly terms with it by picking it up and looking at it from every angle, whereas you can only really get to know a big modern bronze—like Mestrovic's "Moses" on the Notre Dame campus—by climbing all over it with the help of a ladder, which is only allowed on graduation day, and even then only to students.

As we entered a big garden with a tiny cor-

beled cottage and an enormous studio, Miss Holt's next door neighbor, who turned out to be the Anglican vicar's wife, offered to go in search of the sculptor. I thanked her gratefully because I anticipated that my hostess would be hard at work carving until the minute of my scheduled arrival, and probably oblivious to everything else except the sculpture on hand. Carving is an absorbing discipline that demands not merely hard work, but complete concentration—unless you want a cut finger.

When Miss Holt finally appeared in the 16th-

"Girl with Cat," by Gwynneth Holt.

century doorway and let me in I was too impressed by the interior to say very much for a moment or two. Here was the sort of ambience that would suit even the most fastidious of artists. The plain whitewash and black oak beams of the interior were set off by the sculptor's own creamy colored ivory carvings, displayed on natural wood brackets. Although there was an Eric Gill etching on the wall, most of the treasures on display were anything but modern. There was a Rembrandt print, a Tanagra figurine, a stone head of a god broken from some Indian temple, and some fine Chinese ivories. These influences from past cultures were reinforced by the books on the shelf, books about ancient Egyptian and Assyrian sculpture. Ivory carvers are much more influenced by antiquity than those who work in some other material. A contemporary ivory carver such as Richard Robertson of Aberdeen, for example, will remark that he owes everything to the Romanesque Period, in the way that a figurative bronze sculptor might say that he was a follower of Henry Moore. Whereas most of the textures of modern sculpture have changed with new surface finishes, plastics, and new kinds of metal for casting, ivory looks just as it did when Our Glorious Founders, the new stone age sculptors, set about chipping it with flint knives. Nor, for that matter, has the shape of the material changed: a slice down the middle of a tusk will still give you the basic shape of a consular diptych; a statue carved from the whole tusk has still got to sway slightly in one direction, and thus inevitably suggest a Romanesque or Medieval prototype.

Over lunch (which was eaten with knives whose handles were made of elephant's teeth) Gwynneth Holt told me that she felt she had no difficulty in carrying on from where the last religious ivory sculptors in Britain left off, at the time of the Reformation. She explained how she had developed as a carver—like so many British ivory sculptors, she is self-taught.

"If you can carve anything you can carve in ivory. When my first husband and I were students at Wolverhampton School of Art, we were

"Gabriel," by Richard Robertson.

both interested in trying to carve ivory. We found a small shop in the town owned by a very old man who was famous for making billiard balls. He was then too old to work very much and spent most of his time sitting on a chair in his doorway with a red handkerchief round his neck. We used to talk to him and became very friendly. He enjoyed our interest in ivory and showed us some of his work. Among his billiard balls there were some birds cut out with a lathe, which he was very proud of and which we admired very much; a great achievement and well done. We bought some small pieces of ivory from him and then some engravers' files, etc., and started in small figures for pendants, rings, etc. This soon led us to doing larger work and we had to find somewhere to buy tusks. The antique shops in those days supplied our needs, and eventually the old man disappeared and we moved to Scotland. I was very interested in Chinese carvings and perhaps in the early days slightly influenced, but my greatest pleasure was the medieval carvings, particularly those of the 12th to the 14th century. I was very keen on developing a style of my own, if I have succeeded, I do not know.

"I give a great deal of thought to the material, in which way to use it best. It is so beautiful in itself and I try not to destroy this. I am sometimes governed by its shapes and curves, but I feel less strongly than I did at one period that I must keep all my carvings to the shape of the tusk, because I have thought of various ways of bypassing the basic shape. Look at that statue of Pope John for example, and the other one of Christ entering Jerusalem. They were both made by sawing the hollow end of the tusk, what I call 'the can,' lengthways and using the different halves for two quite unrelated works."

As we made a tour of the cottage, I thought that because an ivory carver's works are always small enough to go on display in his own home he will always be much more influenced by his own sculpture than a worker in some other medium. His style may become more consolidated, but it is much more likely that he will

Finished carving for "The Entering into Jerusalem." The donkey's ears are a much less prominent feature in the carving than in the original maquette.

react against his earlier work and start to work in a different way, like Wilhelm Wegel, for instance. Some of the ivory sculptures on view in the various rooms were by Gwynneth Holt's husband, Thomas Bayliss Huxley Jones. There was more than a passing resemblance between the husband's and wife's work, and I felt that it was probably impossible for ivory sculptors to work in close proximity without modifying one another's styles. Resemblances between sculptors of the same "school" of ivory carving, such as Stephany and Dresch, are probably due to un-

"Angel," by Thomas Bayliss Huxley Jones.

conscious assimilation as much as conscious imitation.

We went out into the large studio in the garden, which I had assumed would be Miss Holt's, but it had been her husband's. This garden studio, she explained, was cold and drafty in winter, and she preferred to work indoors. It was easier to keep ivory at the right condition in the cold. Once, when her husband was artist-in-residence at Dartmouth College, Hanover, New Hampshire, she had begun carving some ivory that kept dehydrating in the centrally heated studio, and consequently splitting. Finally she hit on the idea of smearing it with cold cream to keep it moist. At this point Miss Holt opened the door of what had obviously been a powder closet in the 18th century. It was a small room, opening off the living room and looking directly onto the street, with two windows giving the essential side light onto the work bench. Here was where she did all her carving.

I looked round. Apart from the stout wooden bench, with its two vises—one with claws, the other with a leather lining to prevent the ivory from slipping—and the neat wooden boxes to hold the tools, this room looked more like a shrine than a studio. There were religious statues in ivory standing here and there, and maquette studies in plasticine for other carvings.

Miss Holt had apologized for the mess, but I couldn't see any. There were no chippings to be seen, no ivory, and even the floorboards, darkened and polished with age and use, had been swept immaculately. The sculptress started pulling out the drawers that lined one side of the room and showed me her stock of ivory: African and Indian elephant tusks, hippopotamus' teeth, whales' teeth, even walrus tusks. She

The Genesis of an Ivory Carving, Maquettes. These sketch models in modeling clay show the original ideas for "Guinea Pig," "Family Group," and "The Entering into Jerusalem."

wasn't sure whether the tusk she was showing me was from a boar or not. I reflected that as long as you can carve it, one kind of ivory is rather like another to an ivory sculptor, and that the references often seen in art books or museums, to a carving being made from some particular kind of ivory, such as "fossil walrus," are often much more meaningful to economic historians concerned with the movement of trade in the past than to artists. All is grist to the mill.

"Of course," explained the sculptress, "I have much more ivory here than I can ever use." Visits to antique shops and presents from admirers of her work had provided most of it. The average ivory carver does not visit ivory warehouses very much. Miss Holt sounded interested when I told her how ivory merchants lubricate their saws with water when they are cutting ivory. She had obviously never watched this being done and always sawed hers with a dry saw. Of course the second-hand ivory that sculptors do buy is well seasoned, and this may account for the fact that there seem to be fewer cracks in western carvings than those made in countries such as Ceylon or India where fresh ivory is used.

I looked closely at all the sculptress' tools: "I have a vise with jaws in, and that helps to hold the carving," she told me. "But ivory is terribly skiddy stuff, as you must know, and it slips very easily, doesn't it? So it makes it difficult. These vises help to hold it. If I made a plaque I would dig a hole in a piece of wood, push it in, and stick the ivory down in it with shellac.

"I use rasps and files, like these little French files, with rifflers. Some of my tools are home made. To begin with I just bought engraving tools and cut them about a bit. Those tools belonged to Richard Garbe, he gave them to me before he died.

"I cut up the tusk with a cabinet maker's saw, or a bow saw. I always start by cutting off as much as I can, so as not to waste the ivory. I begin by making drawings and sketches of the figure I want to carve, and then from that I do a plasticine model to the scale I want and then

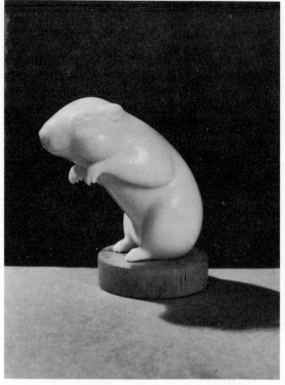

The Finished Carving of "Guinea Pig."

work from it. Then I chip off the rough bits and gradually work down to cutting and filing and scraping until the carving works up to a polish. I don't like them scraped down too much, I prefer to see a little bit of cutting left in them in places so that you can see how they have been constructed by the tool marks. I polish the ivory with soap powder and a piece of felt. I don't like them too highly polished anyway because they always come up much more, don't they?"

I asked her how long it took to make one of her large carvings. "It's awfully difficult to say. It's really much slower than carving in other materials, like wood and stone, and I think that's why it isn't used so much. It takes me quite a few months, anyway. I couldn't possibly do it in weeks. Another thing is that I don't like to be rushed on carvings, and I find that once I've got the rough part off and started going it's sometimes better to leave them and come back to them; you find you get on so much better,

"Our Lady," by Gwynneth Holt.

marble as well. "Well, you can't earn your living by ivory carving, can you? The cost of ivories is obviously dictated by the time spent on them, and I think it's true to say that although ivory carvings are expensive, they don't really pay the sculptor for the time he puts into them, because there is a terrific amount of work in them."

I reflected that ivory carvings were an expensive luxury that flourished during periods of prosperity. English squires and clergymen could afford to buy the very highly priced ivory ships made by American prisoners during the War of 1812 because British agriculture was prospering. When the Depression arrived in 1929, Otto Glenz had been forced to give up carving large ivories because no one would buy them. Since the 18th century at least, ivory carvers have complained that they did not get enough for their labors. Almost the first reference to the Dieppe ivory carvers was a statement by the historian of their town that they made magnificent carvings but were not paid well enough for them. I had in my pocket a letter from one of the last two Dieppe carvers, saying he had been forced to lower his prices because of competition from Hong Kong and because he could no longer find patrons who appreciated fine workmanship.

"Of course," said Miss Holt, "people always will go on carving ivory, you know." I agreed with her; there is an attraction about ivory carving that has nothing to do with material rewards, or even with artistic fame. The cavemen must have felt it when they experimented with man's first artistic material, mammoth ivory. Amateurs have always been drawn toward ivory, like the first scrimshoners of the 17th century, and its attraction is still as real today as it has ever been. Miss Holt asked whether I had done much carving lately. I defensively replied that I had been very busy with my book. Of course it had been very helpful to me, as an ivory sculptor, to find out about the work of so many other carvers. I pointed to a flower carving that she had just made and said that was the sort of thing I meant. No one in England had ever made any flower sculpture in ivory before she had, and it

because you can get quite stale going on all the time at the same thing, especially a thing that's rather finicky to do."

I asked whether it was in order to get a change that so many ivory carvers worked in bronze and

Figure A

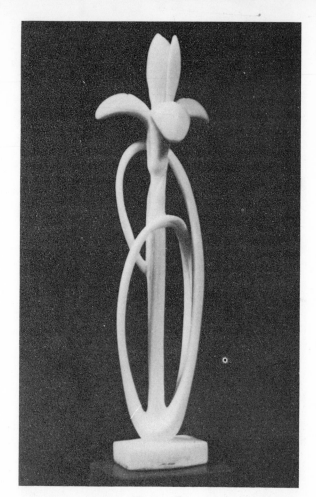

Figure B

Flower pieces by Gwynneth Holt. Figure D appears in the first illustration on Gwynneth Holt's studio bench as a piece of ivory marked out for carving.

Figure C

Figure D

Figure E

showed how even such a well-used art form as ivory carving was far from being exhausted.

It was impossible to appreciate any modern form of art unless it could be compared with what had gone before, I said. Now the materials for just such a comparison had been entirely lacking before I had begun this book. Modern ivory carving had been sneered at as not worth the trouble of study, yet some of the greatest carvings had been made in quite modern times. I hoped that this book would make people take more interest in the ivory carving of other countries, because it was related to their own. The basic style of much French ivory carving, *mosaique,* could now be shown to have come to France from Siberia via Russia. France in turn had contributed the rose motif to Germany. Students of American art would now become much more interested in 17th century English folk art forms because scrimshaw, which was supposed to be an indigenous American folk art of the early 19th century, could now be shown to have been made by English whalers from Hull in the 17th century. English collectors who had paid thousands of dollars for ivory ship models, under the impression that they were made by French prisoners, would now have to face up to the fact that many of them must have been made by Americans, who had thus put themselves on a level with the cleverest professional ivory carvers Europe could produce.

It had all been very interesting, I concluded.

Just the same I had an exhibition in the offing, my tools and the piece of ivory waiting for me and it would be nice to get back to my bench and there.

Modern Ivory Carving

Chapter 1.

How an Improved Supply of Ivory Affected Ivory Sculpture

During the early years of the 19th century the amount of ivory imported to America and England, the two countries taking the bulk of African and Asiatic ivory, had been very small. In 1827, for example, less than one ton was imported into England.[1] By the middle of the century, however, the demand for "white gold," as it was called at the time, had quickened considerably. By 1851, the year of the Great Exhibition, 302 tons were imported to London, and for the rest of the century there was never a year when less than 400 tons of tusks were unloaded at London docks, while the figure frequently rose above 600.

The same rise in ivory imports held good in America, where a visitor to Grote and Co., the principal ivory importer of New York, saw stacks of tusks six inches in diameter, newly arrived consignments of ivory still wrapped in the rawhide "schroons" or parcels in which they had been encased in the West African jungles, and assortments of every conceivable kind of ivory, from the pinkish hued Indian to the thick enameled Abyssinian. Appropriately enough, the shop

sign of this leading American importer was a tusk nine feet long.

Other important ivory ports were Hamburg, which took the ivory of the German Cameroons, tusks that vied with those of the Siamese elephant for pride of place as the best quality ivory obtainable anywhere, and Antwerp, which took the rising output of the newly opened Belgian Congo. It was imports of ivory to the latter port that were going to have the most formative effect on the development of ivory sculpture, by promoting the rise of the Belgian school of carvers, who were, in turn, to affect radically ivory sculpture in France and England.

In view of the large imports of ivory into the United States during the 19th century, it is rather regrettable that Abraham Lincoln should have refused the generous offer made by the King of Siam to give a stud of elephants to America.

The master of a United States sailing ship, the *John Adams,* Captain Berrien by name, had to pay his respects to the King. During their conversation, the monarch had been much struck by the fact that there were no elephants in the United States, although Americans regarded them with great interest and would always flock to see one on display. His Majesty immediately

---

1. According to the American author, C. F. Holder, *Ivory King,* but Alfred Ogle Maskell (Encyclopaedia Britannica, 1911, p. 93) gives a much higher figure—150 tons.

dictated a letter to the President of the United States. The epistle, dated "Fifth night of the Waxing Moon, in the lunar month from the commencement of the cold season in the Year of the Monkey, given in our royal audience hall, the Grand Palace, Bangkok," offered to give a number of young elephants of both sexes to America if the United States would provide shipping.

He pointed out, very sensibly, that the trip had better be made by steamer, rather than sailing vessel, so that the elephants would arrive in good condition. Elephants transplanted well, the King added; they had been taken to Ceylon in the 15th century, and had thriven there. "If on the continent of America," said the King, "there should be several pairs of young male and female elephants turned loose in forests, where there was abundance of water and grass, in any region called by the English the torrid zone, and all were forbidden to molest them, We are of the opinion, that after a while, they will increase till there be large herds, as there are on the continent of Asia, until the inhabitants of America will be able to catch them and tame them, and use them as beasts of burden, because on account of the great strength and size of the elephants, they could be made to carry very heavy loads, and would be of benefit to the country, since they can travel where carriage and other roads have not been made."

The King sealed the letter, which was inscribed on gilt-edged paper, with his personal seal, enclosed it in a bag of cloth of gold, locked it in a gilded box, and handed it to the courier. Then no doubt he stroked the mat on which he sat, which like all the royal mats, was made of minute strips of ivory bound with gold leaf, and reflected on the princely generosity of his offer.

Siamese ivory has long been esteemed as the finest and purest ivory obtainable. For years I regretted that I could not obtain any (for it is all consumed in the country of origin) and now that someone has kindly given me a pair of Siamese tusks I feel I shall never be able to make anything worthy of the material. Moreover, to the

Siamese, the elephant is not merely a kingly beast (all elephants are a royal prerogative and the monarch claims descent from the offspring of a princess and an elephant) but a divine one as well. Buddha's mother was impregnated by the touch of an elephant's trunk, and from among the ranks of the forest elephants there emerged, every so often, the White Elephant, symbol of the Living Buddha.

So the King was not merely offering to present the American people with unlimited supplies of the best ivory obtainable, but giving them something of his family and his god as well. He may well have stressed the wideness of his generosity to the royal governess, Anna Leonowens (of "Anna and the King of Siam" fame), who had composed the "true translation into English" that accompanied the letter. The king was a great patron of the arts and had despatched mother-of-pearl carvers from the royal household to the Paris Exhibition of 1867, suggesting to them, when the Parisians showed little appreciation of their carvings of scenes from the life of Buddha, that they should sculpt some Christian themes instead. So he must have known all about the value of Siamese ivory.

In view of the fact that the Americans were busy trying to acclimatize camels to their desert (which Captain Berrien had mentioned to the King), there was nothing of a particularly hair-brained nature about this attempt to raise a native breed of elephants.

It is possible to visualize the consequence of just such a stock of American elephants, with emigrants crossing the plains in howdahs on their backs, secure from Indian attack because horses hate the smell of tuskers and the Indians could never have induced their Appaloosas to approach the strange beasts. Elephants would have been equally useful in the forests of the Old Northwest, rolling and hauling logs and pushing down trees with their foreheads. As a fringe benefit, there would have been an abundant supply of political mascots.

The letter, which was dated, in our style, 14th February, 1861, did not take long to reach

Abraham Lincoln, and was as promptly replied to. The President politely declined. "What shall I do if the King *has* sent off the elephants before he gets your letter and they arrive in Washington?" Secretary of State Seward asked Lincoln.

"Use them to stamp out the rebels" was the reply.

The great bulk of the increased imports of ivory was pouring into America and Europe from Africa, a country from which floods of the precious material had been released, by the middle of the 19th century, through the activities of missionaries and colonizers.

In East Africa, ivory had always been very much associated with the slave trade, because the tusks were brought from the interior by the slaves who were being marched to the coast for shipment from Zanzibar. The larger tusks were carried by men, the smaller "scrivelloes," which were destined to be turned into billiard balls, by women and children. Although my daughter (aged eight) can pick up and carry a full-grown elephant's tusk (weighing 22 pounds), it is quite another matter to carry even a small tusk on successive days' marches through the African bush. Many women and children failed to keep up with the slave column and were shot by their Arab captors, or tied to trees and left for the hyenas to tear them to bits at nightfall. By making an example of the laggards, the slave dealers would encourage the others to keep up their due speed. Transport of this sort meant that the price of ivory was human blood, and humanitarians like Dr. Livingstone were very keen to open *direct* communication with the African interior, preferably by means of steamboats on a navigable waterway. Much of the "River Searcher's" explorations, to give Livingstone his native name, were concerned with finding just such a water-borne means of shipping ivory to the coast. If the slavers could be deprived of their ivory, more than half their profit would be gone, and the whole trade would probably die out.

Moreover, it was not just the Arabs who hunted slaves; some of the greatest hunters were particular African tribes, like the Makololo, Livingstone's greatest friends. If only these Africans could be persuaded to abandon the trade in human beings for the "legitimate trade" of ivory, the slave trade would be about halved.

To the average African the tusks of an elephant are a mere adjunct to a meat meal, like the wishbone of a turkey. They are difficult to work, difficult to transport, and often a prerogative of the local chief—anyone who attempted to conceal the discovery of a pair of tusks would receive a punishment from his chief, which made the atrocities of the slave traders appear anemic. Africans have produced some wonderful ivory sculpture, but then they can produce equally good sculpture in all sorts of out-of-the-way materials, such as dried blood. Most tribes that acquired ivory before the days of communications with the coast did not know what to do with it. They surrounded their chiefs' huts with fences of ivory tusks, or the chief would heap them in a corner of his hut, bury them under the floor, or conceal them in the thatch of the roof.

Once regular communications with the exterior had been established, however, and European merchants had begun to penetrate the country, this hoarded ivory was released, and the gas pipe-gun that a chief would obtain for 120 pounds of ivory would be used to kill more elephants. This was an addition to the traditional hunting methods, which included an attack by mounted hunters who would encircle the beast and hamstring it with long swords, killing it with poisoned spears or arrows, or transfixing it with a deadfall spear, a giant weapon suspended over an elephant track by a forest liana strung between two tree trunks. The thrust of the elephant's shoulders against the tightly stretched liana was sufficient to break it and send the monster spear crashing into its spine.

It was not necessary to kill an elephant to collect its tusks. A dead or dying elephant would reveal its presence by the clouds of birds surrounding it. Contrary to popular belief, elephants are no more forewarned of the moment of their passing than other mortals, and far from depositing their tusks in an "elephant's graveyard" they would probably die on the elephant track they were following, making it easy for the hunters who were following that path to collect their ivory. Returns from the ivory trade indicate that four-fifths of the ivory sold during the 19th century had been picked up in this way.

Although African hunters, with their spears and gas pipe-guns, probably always accounted for the bulk of the kills, white hunters also enjoyed a brief but successful heyday. They appeared in the wake of the missionaries, who were frequently instrumental in persuading chiefs to forego their cherished royal prerogative of monopolizing ivory and to welcome the newcomers. Some hunters, like Henry Hartley, became close friends of the African rulers; others, such as Frederick Courtney Selous, the most famous of them all, carried out valuable work as explorers as well as hunters.

The white hunters began by attacking the elephant on horseback and riding through the herd, shooting as many as they could. Elephants soon became more wary and short in supply, however, and it was then necessary to track them through the thick forest, a much more difficult and dangerous task. At first the hunters were armed with enormous guns firing heavy charges—Sir Samuel Baker used a colossal weapon that weighed 21 pounds, took 16 drams of powder to load, and fired a conical bullet weighing four ounces. The stocks of these weapons were bound with pieces of rawhide taken from the elephant's ear so as to strengthen them and minimize the chances of a burst barrel. Gradually it was discovered that a small bullet would do the work of a large one, and one well placed bullet the work of two from a double-barreled gun that were not aimed directly at the brain or the heart. Hunters abandoned the double-barreled guns (which were often shotguns with shortened barrels) and black powder in favor of an ever decreasingly sized rifle with a nitro catridge.

Soon a single Dutch expedition might bring back 10,000 pounds of ivory in its game bag, while an individual hunter might kill 14 elephants a day, or 133 on a single trip.

Only a very small portion of the ivory that was flooding out of Africa was used by ivory sculptors. The bulk of it went to manufacturers who produced billiard balls, knife handles, and hairbrushes. Much of the ivory imported to New York during the 19th century was sawn into slabs and sent to Sheffield, from where it would return to America in the shape of knife handles. Then, as later, it is very doubtful if the demands of ivory sculptors caused a slaughter of elephants. The elephant is a voracious feeder who spoils what he does not eat. He has always been a foe of agriculturists, right through history, and the Ceylon elephant, which is almost always tuskless, has been just as depredated as other breeds. Anyone who looks into an ivory warehouse today will see bundles of baby elephant tusks. These immature beasts have not been shot for their ivory, as they yield so little that it would obviously have been in the hunter's interest to let them grow to adulthood, but as part of a cropping process whereby the new African states are attempting to decrease their elephant population and increase their human one. As Oscar Wilde said of the wallpaper in the bedroom of the Paris hotel in which he died: "One of us will have to go."

If the bulk of ivory went for industrial purposes, how could increased supplies of tusks have any effect on ivory sculpture?

Although ivory sculpture is a miniature art, ivory is a resplendent material, and the more of it there is to reflect light, the more successful an impression does it make. The tusks available to artists in the 18th century appear very small in comparison with the really huge ones that now came on the market. The Victorians loved size for its own sake, and they flocked to see large ivory exhibits, such as the giant Sheffield penknife on view at the Great Exhibition of 1851. This had a handle five feet long, carved from a single tusk; it is still in existence. Probably exhibits of this sort attracted much more attention than did the delicate filagree ivory carvings of French sculptors of the 18th century who had been obliged to work from much smaller sections.

Dieppe and other existing ivory carving centers were able to continue and expand to meet the needs of a growing population. By 1840, for example, Dieppe had no fewer than 11 ivory *ateliers,* many more than had existed during Napoleonic times. Ehrbach in Germany was also able to expand.

The increased output of purely utilitarian objects, such as the ivory doorknobs beloved by 19th-century America and England (Queen Victoria even ordered them for the doors of the royal train), may have resulted in a greater taste

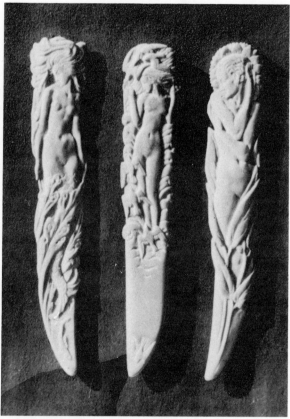

"Sea Maiden," "Aphrodite," and "Clytie," by M. Joyce Bidder. The Arts and Crafts Movement of the late 19th century destroyed the distinction between ivory carving for the exhibition and the making of functional ivories. Many contemporary English ivories are designed with a purpose in mind, like these paper knives.

for more artistic and less utilitarian ivory carvings. Indeed it is difficult to draw a precise line between ivory sculpture and craftsmanship, nor should one try to do this, because they interact. For example, M. Joyce Bidder, a distinguished English ivory sculptor, only took to ivory because she found in an attic the ivory rulers that had belonged to her grandfather, a Victorian civil engineer.

But the biggest effect of increased ivory production is to be found in the efforts made by King Leopold of the Belgians to stimulate the demand for one of the products of his newly acquired personal domain, the Congo. So as to promote an interest in ivory sculpture he gave various well-known Belgian sculptors the largest and best tusks that had so far come out of the "Free State."

Forty ivory sculptors sent work to be shown at the Brussels Exhibition of 1887, more ivories than had ever been on exhibition at any one time before. Many of the exhibitors have dropped out of public acclaim, even in the country of their origin, but the year 1887 remains a momentous one in the history of the art.

The sculptors had to solve the problem of creating free-standing sculptures, of dimensions sufficiently large to approach to, or at least suggest, the pieces normally shown in the *salons.* Only a few, such as Constantin Meunier and Egide Rombaux, were content to carve their figures from a tusk, or to do some carpentry and have an ivory figure with attached ivory arms. The rest, including such influential sculptors as Julien Dillens, Charles Van der Stappen, Philippe Wolfers, and Charles Samuel, contributed what were essentially *composite* sculptures, in which ivory was mixed with some other substance, such as bronze, marble, silver-gilt, enamel, or jewels. In some entries, such as that of Fernand Khnopff, the role that ivory played in the exhibit was merely a token one; it was reduced to a piece of inlay, such as a face in an otherwise all bronze composition.

Composite ivory sculpture would have been impossible had not the scramble for Africa

A bust in ivory of King Leopold II by the Belgian sculptor Thomas Vinçotte. (*Musée Royal*)

This medallion, of African ivory embedded in an ebony plaque, symbolizes the arrival of white colonialism in black Africa, and one of the results, the revival of ivory sculpture in Belgium, as a consequence of better supplies of raw ivory. By the Belgian sculptor Floris de Cuyper, probably about 1912. Note the tusk that the personification of the Congo holds. (*Musée Royal de l'Afrique Centrale,* Tervuren, Belgium)

brought the thicker tusks that have already been referred to, such as the nine-foot-long ivory sign used by Grote and Company on 14th Street, New York City.

It would have taken a tusk of quite these dimensions to have supplied the ivory sections of Sir George Frampton's "Lamia," Sir W. Reynold Stephen's "Guinevere And The Nestling," or Théodore Rivière's "Salammbo Before Matho." All these are virtually life-size figures.

The reasons for the preference of the Brussels exhibitors for composite sculpture as opposed to what Dunstan Pruden, in a review of one of my books, called "The essentially three-dimension tusk," are not hard to find. Although to a purist like Pruden, sculpture wrenched from the spatial boundaries of the tusk may well seem "perversion," sculpture within the confines of a tusk imposes its own limitations. "I keep all my sculpture within the limitations of the natural tusk," Jeanne Bell told me, "though that makes it more difficult to think of fresh designs."

Many of the exhibitors had made their name in other materials—Dillens, for example, was well known for his statues and fountains. To such artists the temptation to use ivory as just another adjunct to sculpture, like a bronze wreath added to a marble statue, was irresistible. One of Dillens' exhibits, "Glory," even has a metal wreath added to the head of the figure, whereas the whole composition would have been far more effective if the wreath had been carved from the ivory surrounding the head.

Because ivory sculptors have often been closely associated with goldsmithery as well, it was perfectly natural that a goldsmith-turned-ivory-sculptor such as Phillippe Wolfers should ex-

hibit at Brussels his "Fairy with a Peacock," in which ivory is combined with silver-gilt, opals, and translucent enamels.

What was more, it seemed natural to people so imbued with the classics as the Belgians to

"Lamia," by Sir George Frampton.

Sir Alfred Gilbert. Figure for the Duke of Clarence's tomb, Albert Memorial Chapel, Windsor Castle, England. Note the downcast eyes. (Reproduced by gracious permission of Her Majesty the Queen)

"Salaambo Before Matho," by Theodore Rivière. Composition sculpture at its best. The ivory and bronze seem to melt together. Luxembourg Palace, Paris, France.

"Guinevere and the Nestling," by Sir William Reynolds Stephens. No European artist has ever captured the spirit of Arthurian Romance so well as this Detroit-born sculptor.

revive the combined gold and ivory sculpture of the Greeks and Romans. There was a good deal of difference between the two attempts at the same medium, however. An ivory statue of Athene, to which removable gold drapery has been added, which can be melted down at a time of national crisis, and an ivory and silver gilt statue, in which the ivory is likely to be marked by the tarnishing of the silver, are two quite separate art forms.

The decision of so many sculptors at Brussels in 1887 to send in combination sculpture was to have a profound effect. The lead that Belgium had given was to be followed by France ("the strongest of the Gauls are the Belgians," as Julius Caesar remarked) and by Britain. Combination sculpture was to continue in vogue at least until the *Art Nouveau* period, and but for Richard Garbe and the English School it might well be the main medium of ivory carving today.

Chapter 2.

American Ivory Carving: Scrimshaw

Between the beginning of the 19th century and its last quarter American ivory carving underwent two periods of intense activity. During the first, which lasted roughly between 1812 and 1815, American prisoners of war penned up in British camps made ivory and bone ship models; in the second, which stretched between 1800 and 1880, the artists of the forecastle aboard American whalers raised scrimshaw to one of the great art forms of the world.

Outside of these two great bursts of creative activity ivory carving is dormant, but the full years make up for the lean ones that follow during the later 19th and the 20th centuries because both these sets of ivory carvings constitute the earliest American art products to be widely appreciated, and collected, outside of American soil. This recognition by foreign connoisseurs marks, as it were, the coming of age of American art.

The two spells of activity in ivory carving—a spring and summer that had no autumn—are not so unrelated as might appear at first sight. The resemblance between the wooden prison huts of Dartmoor and the cramped forecastle of a whaler is inescapable. The claustrophobic conditions of prison, no less than life on shipboard (which as Herman Melville has rightly pointed out tended to make men revert to the state of the savage), must have recalled the caves of the New Stone

Age where man had first crossed the line that separates the brute from humanity by engraving a scrimshaw line on a mammoth's tusk. But although the exceptional conditions of life on a whaler or in the dungeon of an English castle may have awakened latent ancestral memories of primitive skills, there were other and more prosaic reasons for the flowering of American art, which we are about to witness.

Both sets of carvers had almost unlimited time on their hands; it took as long to make a cruise after whales as it did to fight the War of 1812. You cannot hurry a good ivory carving; it is not the sort of thing that you can dash off in a morning's work, like a pencil sketch or an easel painting. Moreover, both sets of carvers had a ready market for their work. The whalers, as will be seen, could sell their products to their shipmates or to dealers in marine curios at the ports where they touched. The prisoners found a ready sale for their wares at the fairs held in their prison camps. Both sets of artists, while not exactly afflicted by dire want, were at least short of most of the necessities and all the luxuries of life, and as Edmond About has pointed out, there is no greater stimulus to an artist than to be hard up. This is why, although few artists ever become millionaires, no millionaire ever wants to become an artist. The necessities and luxuries of life for whalers and prisoners alike were often summed up in one word: tobacco. American prisoners in particular were so addicted to their "chaw" that not merely did the United States government pay them a regular stipend through its prison agent so that they could buy the stuff, but when, as a punitive measure, they were deprived of tobacco by their captors some of them immediately sickened and died in the prison hospital.

But there was a much stronger connection between the two sets of ivory carvers than any we have so far mentioned. This was the fact that prisoners and people on shipboard—passengers as well as crew—were expected to pass the time in whittling something or other. Eric Gill once said that everyone could be an artist if he tried. He demonstrated his point by handing one of his models, who was an actor, a pencil and telling him to draw. The model discovered in himself a talent for drawing that he had never suspected before. This was just what happened in prison camps. Prisoners had always been very much associated with craft work, and particularly sculpture. Macdonald of Keppoch, a Jacobite Highland chief captured during the rising of 1745, covered the walls of his prison in the Keep of Carlisle Castle, with the most elaborate carvings—many of them very plump nudes—which he executed with a nail. It was natural that any prisoner who arrived in a camp and saw all the craft work going on around him should want to join in. It was the same thing aboard ship. The English writer William Makepeace Thackeray was held up in port while his ship went through quarantine formalities. In order to pass the time he began to carve a most elaborate folding toy made from a single piece of wood. When the quarantine was suddenly and unexpectedly lifted he felt aggrieved because he would never have enough leisure to finish his carving.

So in the unusual but stimulating conditions of a whaler or a prison camp many Americans who had never been artists before became adept at ivory carving. But they were temporary sculptors, and once the stimulus was removed few seem to have felt any incentive to go on with their sculpture. Sometimes they could not get the

right material. One modern scrimshaw artist writes to me that he is expecting his next consignment of sperm whale teeth "from South Georgia, via the 'John Biscoe,' who I hope will bring me some this year. They are carefully wrapped, and very bloody and meaty, to say naught of the smell."

This gentleman, Captain Spencer Jones of the yacht *Escape,* is fortunate in that he has good contacts with whalers and the leisure time to carry out his art. The average whale fisherman probably could not look forward to a leisured retirement of this sort however. If he were lucky enough to get home, with savings to live on or relatives to look after him he would still find it difficult to get fresh whale's teeth. Most of them would have been used up on the voyage home. More often a veteran whaler or prisoner would never be able to do any ivory carving because he would have fitted into some job that occupied most of his time. One ex-prisoner, who had lost a leg when the British sentries fired into a crowd of prisoners during a scuffle at Dartmoor, took a job as porter at the Medical College in Washington, D. C. to supplement the pension that the British government gave him as compensation. Obviously he would be too busy welcoming visitors to the College to carry on any of his former prison activities.

Patrons, too, would be wanting. As we shall see in a moment, a piece of New Bedford scrimshaw would sell for a very good price in Dunedin, New Zealand. But it would sell for very much less in New Bedford where there was a lot of it on the market. The American ship modelers had sold their work to English art lovers with plenty of money, clergymen, squires, rich merchants, and well-to-do ladies who felt sorry for the prisoners as well as admiring their handiwork. These patrons, and dealers as well, had come regularly to the prison market, and the prison craftsmen had been able to dispose of their work for very large sums. Once home in America, the carvers might find it much more difficult to come in contact with people with sufficient money to spend on the luxury articles they produced or a taste sufficiently educated to appreciate them.

Thus these two great periods of American ivory carving throw a lot of light not just on American art sculpture but on the production of art works as a whole.

The origin of the word "scrimshaw," which also appears in other forms such as "skrimshander," "scrimshonter," and "scrimshorn," is very obscure. Yet if we only knew what it meant, we would be a lot nearer to discovering how and where the word originated. Ingenious attempts have been made to suggest that it is derived from the need to "scrimp" or save whale's teeth. I have tried to argue elsewhere,[1] however, that there was never any need to economize whale's teeth. A sperm whale was likely to have between 40 to 50 teeth, and a whaler might catch several whales in a day. There ought to have been enough teeth to go round even the most industrious crew without any scrimping, especially as we shall see that making a piece of scrimshaw was a long task that might drag on for months. Although a "skrimshanker" might be a word that could be applied to an idler, this does not seem a very appropriate derivation either. There was nothing about the task of engraving a whale's tooth that suggested idleness; quite the contrary, it meant a lot of hard work.

Scrimshaw is a British surname, not particularly common nowadays (there are only six people of that name in the London telephone directory, which is usually a fairly good index to the frequency of British surnames), but possibly more common in the 19th century. I have argued in the past that the identity of the name of the craft and the surname is too striking to be a coincidence. Scrimshaw may well have been called after a Captain Scrimshaw or harpooner Scrimshaw, who either invented the art or popularized it in the same way that paper cut-outs came to be called by the name of a particular Frenchman, Silhouette.

A British name argues a British invention. I suggested at the time that scrimshaw must have originated in the whalers of Hull and Whitby, in England, and spread to America. One of the discoveries I made while writing this book seems to confirm this supposition. Mr. Edouard A. Stackpoole has pushed back the date of the earliest dated piece of scrimshaw from 1829, which was where it stood when Clifford Ashley began his researches, to 1821. I was able to discover in Hull, England, however, pieces of scrimshaw dated 1665 and 1712. At first sight this appeared to argue strongly for my theory (about the derivation of the word *scrimshaw*) that the art had a British origin. There was one great difficulty about believing this theory completely, however, once more connected with the origin of the word. There can be no doubt that the word "scrimshaw" first appears in America in 1826. On the other hand, in 1853, when the Reverend John Wood wrote his *Illustrated Natural History* in England, he describes scrimshaw, but cannot find a name to call it by. So it seems, regarding derivation, there is still a very strong case to be made for scrimshaw's being a purely native American art form.

Scrimshaw may be defined as carvings or engravings made on shipboard from marine ivory or whalebone. This is an inadequate definition because, as Clifford Ashley pointed out, scrimshaw went through an "Age of Wood" before it reached the "Age of Ivory." His supposition was abundantly confirmed by my discoveries at Hull, which will be described shortly. Whalermen made an enormous variety of scrimshaw, but as we are only concerned with those that are made of ivory, or partly of ivory, it is not necessary to discuss them all, especially as a good deal will be said about the nature of their products when it comes to discussing why they were made.

Instead, I shall try to say something about the origins of scrimshaw, the artists who were concerned with creating it, their motives for working with it, and the methods they used to make it. So much controversy has arisen over all these topics that anyone who attempted to side step

---

1. Carson I. A. Ritchie, *Ivory Carving,* London, 1969.

A photograph of the earliest scrimshaw ever discovered, here published for the first time. These tobacco boxes, made in 1665 (left) and 1712 (right), are made of walrus ivory pegged to a hardwood frame. Their construction bears out Clifford Ashley's prophecy that earlier pieces of scrimshaw than the earliest dated piece (1829) would eventually be found and that scrimshaw must have been made in wood before it was made in ivory. (Museum of Fisheries, Hull, England)

them without discussion might well be accused of attempting to avoid the issues. Moreover, any work of art, even apparently a simple one like a piece of scrimshaw, is a very complex affair, and it is possible to appreciate it to the full only if you know as much about it as can be learned.

There have been many claimants for the honor of originating scrimshaw. Because line engravings on ivory played a large part in the art of the New Stone Age, and reappear in the art of the Eskimo, which resembles strongly Stone Age practice, it seems reasonable to assume that they knew about scrimshaw and practiced it at about the first time the Europeans had any contact with them, which was in the 16th century.

Dr. Frank Boaz,[2] who visited them in 1884, found them making quite complicated scrimshaw with a quartz splinter set firmly in a wooden peg. Once they had got to know the Europeans better, they started using a sharpened nail instead of the stone splinter. This is a very effective tool for making scrimshaw, and as later in the century some whalermen were to make use of it, this seems a definite point of similarity, just as does the use of lampblack for darkening the lines by both sets of artists.

The derivation of this technique from the Eskimos by whalermen has been scouted on the grounds that the eastern Eskimo does very crude work, while the excellent handiwork of the western Eskimo was unknown to whalermen until scrimshaw had reached its full development. The Arctic, moreover, had never been penetrated by a whaler until 1835. Unfortunately for this theory the *central* Eskimo, whose sophisticated techniques were, as has already been said, investigated by Boaz, had long been in contact with European mariners. There is a permanent monument to that contact not half a mile from where I live, in the shape of a number of large black stones built into a crumbling priory wall. This is all that is left of a large cargo of black rock that its discoverer, Sir Martin Frobisher, brought

back from the Arctic in 1578 to Dartford, Kent, England under the enthusiastic belief that it had a high yield of gold. Frobisher (a Yorkshireman) had had many contacts with the Eskimos in his previous voyages of 1576 and 1577. He had taught them how to play football, using the ice floes as a playing field, and no doubt the English explorers had learned something from the Eskimos, especially as they carried off some of their women folk. Such cultural contact as this may have passed scrimshaw from the Eskimos to British seamen, who need not, of course, have been whalermen in the first instance, merely sailors with time on their hands and some ivory to play with. It is striking that, as will be seen in a moment, it is in Sir Martin Frobisher's native county, Yorkshire, that scrimshaw first appears in the succeeding century.

Another strong argument for connecting whalermen scrimshaw with Eskimo scrimshaw is that they look very similar. A ship, drawn by an Eskimo, has that fine rakish look that it has on a whale's tooth graphic. It is even possible for an acknowledged expert like Edouard A. Stackpoole to confuse the two kinds of art, as he does when he assigns a group of miniature seals and other animals to the American scrimshawer when they are in fact made by an Eskimo, as is indicated by their inlaid black eyes and the characteristic circle and dot Eskimo ornamentation that decorates the piece.[3]

It is even possible to find pieces of scrimshaw that have been engraved by an Eskimo on one side and by a Yankee whaler on the other.

After considerable search I was able to find one that showed sufficiently clear American and Eskimo characteristics to be worth using as an illustration. It is a walrus tusk of considerable size, such as those Mrs. Brewster records in her log book of 1848, that were traded by the Es-

---

2. Report of the Bureau of Ethnology, 1884–5, Washington, 1888.

3. "Scrimshaw At Mystic Seaport," The Marine Historical Association, Mystic Connecticut, 1958, p 43. Compare with Stackpoole's illustration one on p. 38 of C.A. Burland's "The Decorative Arts of the Mariner," where a similar piece is shown, which is described as Eskimo.

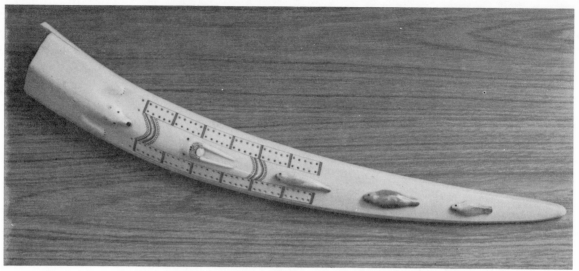

Scrimshaw of mixed Eskimo and American origin. The seals, with their eyes made from plugs of black horn, are characteristically Eskimo. (National Maritime Museum, Greenwich, London)

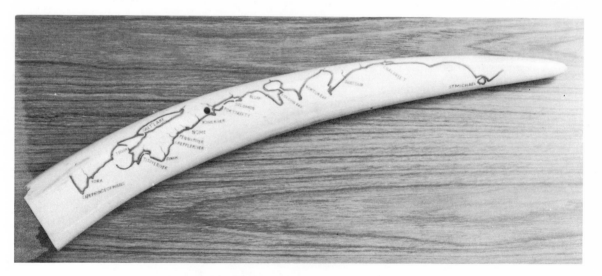

The letters on this scrimshaw map have been cut by someone who was reasonably literate and who was, therefore, more probably an American than an Eskimo. The herringbone border to the map has been cut with a white man's tool—the wood chisel. Note the choice of subject for the carving; cribbage is not an Eskimo game, yet this is undoubtedly a cribbage board. (National Maritime Museum)

kimos of Alaska to American seafarers. There can be little doubt about the characteristic Eskimo decoration of the top of this cribbage board (for that is what the tusk was made into). It has been carved into typically black-eyed Eskimo animals. What convinces me that the bottom of the cribbage board is American work is not merely the clearness of the lettering, which suggests a literate artist, but the rendering of the coastline by "feathering" with a narrow-edged chisel, that is to say rolling the chisel gently from side to side as it is moved along, a process that leaves unmistakable marks and that is made by a tool the Eskimos apparently did not possess, any more than Europeans had developed the technique of inlaying animals' eyes with pieces of black antler. Here then is an example of the sort of work that, much earlier, may have constituted the bridge between Eskimo and American scrimshaw.

There are plenty of other contenders for the honor of having introduced scrimshaw to American whalemen. In the past it was suggested that American seamen learned the arts of ivory carving from the French prisoners with whom they were penned up in prisoner-of-war camps in Georgian England. This is a perfectly valid supposition because the Americans were on good terms with their fellow inmates and learned from them the technique of making ivory ships. It has also been suggested that scrimshaw may have originated in the South Sea Islands. The Polynesians execute darkened line engravings on pearl oyster shell pendants, probably by means of a technique very similar to that used by the whalemen. Neither of these could have produced the rise of scrimshaw, however, because it had begun to develop much earlier.

Art historians have not looked as far afield for the origins of scrimshaw as they might; most of them have been content to assume that it simply originated on the American continent. This is, I feel, a big mistake, and it has arisen from a popular misconception of the American immigrant. Far from being an untutored savage, contemptuous of the finer things that civilization had to offer, settlers in America during the 17th and 18th centuries were often people of the strongest artistic leanings who were determined to endow their adopted country with the best gifts at their disposal. One 18th-century vicar in the backwoods, whose parish was crossed by an Indian war path, and who took an active part in organizing his parishioners in frontier warfare, had nevertheless brought with him—as the inventory of his goods in Lambeth Palace shows—all the apparatus of Georgian elegance. These included still-life paintings to hang on the walls of his cabin, even though still life is hardly the phrase that could be used to describe a frontier parish at that period.

It seems reasonable then, to look for the origins of scrimshaw in the professional and folk art of the 17th and 18th centuries in Europe. Often these arts have left only fragmentary remains so that it is very difficult to establish any links between them and the arts of the whaler.

Perhaps the best contestants, among professional European artists, for the claim of having originated scrimshaw, are the shell engravers of 17th-century Holland. The Bellequin family, artists who had moved from Mainz to Amsterdam because of the religious troubles of the 16th century, became famous for their black line engravings on nautilus shells, mother of pearl, and ostrich eggs. The Bellequin repertoire extended to engraving so many natural objects that it seems almost strange that they did not include whale's teeth, especially as the family had originally been ivory engravers who engraved the ivory plaques with which muskets and pistols were set in black line engravings. Professional ivory engravers are almost equally likely to have originated scrimshaw. There was one particular set of engravers who had an especially strong claim, and they were the makers of ship instruments. Navigational instruments of the 16th and 17th centuries, such as astrolabes, backstaffs, and cross staffs, were often made completely of ivory covered with black line engraving. If there was one particular set of makers of ivory instruments who were ready to move away from Europe for good and practice their arts elsewhere, it was the *cadraniers* of Dieppe. For centuries they had made wonderful compass roses of ivory, embellished with engraved lettering and sometimes pictures as well, all blackened, just like scrimshaw.

Many of these Norman instrument makers were Protestants, and in 1685 Dieppe, like all the other Huguenot towns of France, was swept by a wave of savage persecution. Cavalrymen from the King's army were billeted on Protestants with orders to make their stay as unpleasant for their hosts as possible. Rendered desperate by the sight of their wives and daughters being raped before their eyes and their homes and shops destroyed, many of the Dieppe ivory carvers became converts to Catholicism. Others held out to the last, like one elderly instrument maker who was dragged through the streets of Dieppe at the end of a rope by a dragoon, and only rescued by a neighbor when at the point of death. Many more sought refuge in flight to countries where their fellow religionists had settled, such as England and the New England colonies.

As if to demonstrate their indignation at this ill treatment of the Huguenorts, an Anglo-Dutch fleet, commanded by Admiral Berkeley, dropped anchor off Dieppe in 1694 and bombarded it with high-angle mortars firing explosive shells, a device that meant the gunner's aim was very sketchy, and his missiles were as likely to fall on civilian as military targets. Great indignation was felt by the Dieppois at the employment of this barbarous weapon—especially as it was a French invention –and when the fleet sailed away, Dieppe was reduced to a smoking ruin. A new dispersal of ivory carvers followed.

It can be said with absolute certainty that whoever began scrimshaw in the 17th century must have been in touch with professional ivory carvers and engravers, and must have handled their products daily. No whaler could leave port without instruments, and her men had to be armed with firearms as a protection against the wild bears of the north and the doubtful friendliness of the Eskimos. Masters and men must have been thoroughly well acquainted with the ivory engravings on gunstocks and compasses and they must have seen professional ivory carvers at work when they called to have instruments or firearms repaired.

There is no proof, however, that the origin of scrimshaw came from the products of the professional carver of ivory; it is just as likely to have stemmed from European folk art. It is easier, after all, to envisage a folk artist in the foc'sle of a whaler than a professional one.

In the 17th and 18th centuries those nations of Europe that could obtain marine or fossil ivory had produced thriving peasant ivory carving industries. In Iceland, for example, where the inhabitants were addicted to chess, each peasant patiently carved himself a set of chessmen, carving the King with his cheeks puffed out, blowing his horn, and with his sword by his side. Each chessman was carved "from a fish's tooth,"[4] obviously that of a whale or a walrus. From time to time these visitants from the far north would be swept onto Icelandic shores with the pack ice driven along by winter's storms; then, if there were polar bears amongst the arrivals, the whole district would have to turn out with pikes to kill them.

Although I looked eagerly for chessmen of this sort while in the National Museum at Reykjavik, I could find none to fit the description. This shows how easy it is for whole categories of folk art, which are essential links between one art form and another, to disappear.

A school of folk art ivory carving that has the strongest affinities with scrimshaw is northern Russian peasant carving in fossil ivory. It has even been possible for Helen L. Winslow to mistake the rook from a Russian chess set for a piece of American scrimshaw and to label it as such.[5] Not merely does it seem, from its fluted

4. Bruzen de la Martinière, *Grande Dictionnaire Historique et Geographique,* "Island," Paris, 1768.

5. In "Art And The Seafarer," London, 1968, p. 273. Compare illustration no. 73 in "Severorusskaya Reznaya Kost" 1956, by I.A. Kryukova.

base and its general resemblance to the Russian pieces that I cite, undoubtedly Russian in appearance, the ship, so far as I know, did not find a place in European chessmen at all, though it was invariably used for a rook in Russian sets. Russian ivory engravers originated the olive branch motif, which was later much used in American and British scrimshaw.

What was more, there were two folk arts practiced on ship board that, without being scrimshaw, have obviously got a strong relationship to it: one was tattooing, in which the artist pricked through the lines of a pattern with a needle and then rubbed in a pigment, such as gunpowder, to darken them (this was very like the technique subsequently employed by the 19th-century scrimshoner); the other craft was that of engraving maps on horns, such as buffalo horns, which according to Charles Kingsley was employed by 16th-century English sailors. It is of course a commonplace that such engraved horns, bearing scrimshaw designs, continued to be made into the 19th century, and they will be met again shortly.

There can be no doubt that when the first dated piece of scrimshaw comes to light, it is a piece of genuine folk art, owing nothing to the professional carver. The founder of the study of scrimshaw as an art, Clifford W. Ashley[6]—referring his readers to the oldest piece of dated scrimshaw he knew of, a whale's tooth made on the ship *Susan* off the coast of Japan in 1829—had prophesied that earlier pieces of scrimshaw would be found and that they would be made of wood. In support of this claim he quoted St. John de Crevecoeur, who visited Nantucket in 1782, and commented: "I must confess that I have never seen more ingenuity in the use of the knife; thus the many idle moments of their lives become usefully employed. In the many hours of leisure which their long cruises afford them, they cut and carve a variety of boxes and pretty toys,

in wood, adapted to different uses which they bring home as testimonies of remembrance to their wives and sweethearts." "Toys" is of course used here in its normal 18th-century sense, meaning a curiosity or plaything, not for children, but grownups.

Ashley's prophecy has been abundantly realized by the discovery of the oldest dated pieces of scrimshaw, of mixed ivory and wooden construction, that obviously form a transitional kind of product between the scrimshaw whittled from wood alone (which he argues, I think rightly, must have been the very earliest attempt at this art) and the more sophisticated attempts in ivory.

The two pieces of scrimshaw have been preserved in the Museum of Fisheries at Hull, England, along with many other relics of the English whaling industry, which was centered on that port. They are made of hard wood, mixed with sections of walrus tusk. The tops and bottoms of the boxes consist of thin pieces of wood, fastened to the sides by small wooden pegs. One box is ornamented by an oval plate of walrus ivory crudely ornamented with milled oval lines in pairs. Within the innermost pair of lines are the letters M.S. and the date 1712. The second example has the top of the box elaborately decorated with nine pieces of ivory, the center one being lozenge shaped and bearing the initials T.F. and the date 1665. Mr. John Bartlett, the Director of the Museum of Fisheries, was good enough to examine the boxes and report on their authenticity to me. "The two snuff boxes," he says, "certainly correspond in make and style to the dates enscribed." Although Mr. Bartlett describes the boxes as snuff boxes, in an earlier catalogue they have been described as patch boxes. These were the boxes in which 18th-century ladies kept the artificial black spots they stuck here and there on their faces. One lady who appeared before the Shah of Persia ornamented in this way was later visited by that monarch's personal physician, at the latter's request, so that he might cure her of the painful disease from which she appeared to be suffering. It would be very interesting if these boxes were patch boxes, because they would be the first in

6. Clifford W. Ashley, *The Yankee Whaler,* London, 1926, pp. 115, 110. The whale's tooth he mentions is now in the Nantucket Historical Association Collection.

a long series of sailors' presents for their sweethearts which is going to crop up again and again in our discussion of scrimshaw. The mottos on the boxes, however, make it almost certain that they are tobacco boxes. One of them bears the legend: "If you love me lend me not" and the other apparently has had a similar motto, in a rather corrupted form. Somehow this seems much more appropriate to a snuff box or tobacco box that is lent about than a patch box that stays on the dressing table.

It is worthwhile making one or two comments about these boxes. The fact that they are tobacco boxes is in itself worth noting. There was nothing more characteristic of a seaman than his tobacco box; the poet Southey, who had befriended a marine, was with difficulty persuaded to accept his box, the man's one possession. The fact that these are initialed suggests that they were made by an individual for his own use. Their rough fastening together argues that they were homemade, and the use of walrus ivory indicates that they were made by a visitor to the Arctic. The fact that they have come to rest with so many other whaling relics suggests that they originated on a whaler. The two boxes, though made at different times, are obviously related to one another.

It would seem, then, that here we have a school of scrimshaw established in the English whaling port of Hull just 164 years before the first piece of American scrimshaw to which a date can be put. It therefore appears possible that scrimshaw is not of American origin at all, but that it crossed the Atlantic with the British whalers who were sent to set up whaleries in America, such as that established by William Penn in 1699. On the other hand, as so many American whalers at one time or another sailed from British ports, one of them might have brought the art with him to England and introduced it here. In some ways the enquiry as to who originated scrimshaw is an irrelevant one. "It does not belong to a particular race or country, but is the property of mankind," as the Marquis of Hastings said of the Taj Mahal. In

other ways, however, the enquiry is extremely relevant, because it is only if the existence of a strong school of British scrimshaw is allowed that it will be possible to sort out the different kinds of artifacts produced by scrimshoners and assign them to an American or a British source.

Until recently the existence of British scrimshaw was a sort of artistic heresy. American writers either assumed that it did not exist, or if they knew of its existence made no reference to it. British and Commonwealth writers did not show as much reticence however. The Tasmanians revealed the extent of their scrimshaw treasures, many of which had been made by British whalemen operating in Australian waters (though some, as will be seen, were American), and John Beckwith suggested that scrimshaw was engraved "by whale fishermen of American and Anglo-American origin."

A strong argument for the British origin of much scrimshaw could have been made from the designs with which it was decorated: these included Britannia, the British lion, or some other national symbol, such as the foul anchor of the Admiralty. It was not advisable to press this line of argument too far, particularly because many pieces of scrimshaw were deliberately given an international style of decoration. They would combine decorative symbols belonging to more than one country so that, wherever they were sold their purchaser would find something to identify himself with his purchase. Nor was it safe to rely on any decorative motifs that could be associated with any pieces of scrimshaw that were known to be British, because the scrimshaw artist was very catholic in his style and made use of forms of decoration also employed by the artists of other countries. What test then could determine whether a particular piece was British or not? Very occasionally a piece of British scrimshaw came provided with a pedigree. Commander Naish was given a scrimshawed whale's tooth by an old lady whose father had been the vicar of Burstead. It had been sent home to her by her sailor sweetheart before he died at sea and kept by her ever since.

Occasionally, too, a piece of scrimshaw bears an inscription that refers to a British ship—"The *Pacific* whaling ship, Captain Robert Gardiner of Hobart Town, homeward bound, 900 barrels sperm oil, 10 months out, 1848."

It is not difficult to see why there should be such a mystery about British scrimshaw. Britain had a considerable whaling fleet, but most of it was engaged in the North Sea fishery off Greenland. Consequently there are comparatively few sperm whale tooth graphics, because the sperm whale is caught mostly south of the Line. Many of the pieces of scrimshaw made by British whalers operating in the South Sea fishery (where it will be remembered the *Pequod* had her famous gam with the British whaler *Samuel Enderby*) have remained in Australasia where, until comparatively recently, little attention was paid to them.

Most striking of all is the fact that English literature is almost dumb about British scrimshaw. The only reference I have been able to find is a chance remark in a book by R. M. Ballantyne, *Fighting the Whales* (1884), who says that seamen aboard whalers save sharkskin so as to use it for sandpaper for "various things they make out of whale's bones and teeth."

It is a striking fact that scrimshaw continued to be made by British whalers for a very long time. British ships, such as those owned by Salveson of Leith, continued to put to sea in pursuit of whales until well into living memory. Indeed

American or British scrimshaw? Only the pursuing whaleboats with sails set give the clue that this is American and not made by British whalers operating off Australian waters. The latter used only oars when closing on a whale. Scrimshaw became the first American art form to be widely bought and appreciated by non-Americans. This piece has been bought by a British patron. (Museum of Fisheries, Hull, England)

British scrimshaw may have gone on far longer than the American variety. Two sea captains to whom I applied for information about how scrimshaw was actually made were able to give me details of the methods that had been used up to the last days of British whaling, while one of them, I am glad to say, is still making scrimshaw.

One of the consequences of the confusion that has arisen between American and British scrimshaw is that many collectors and museums in America have acquired British pieces that have been classified as American. "Ninety percent of the old 'real' U.S.A. scrimshaw," Captain Spencer Johnson of the yacht *Escape* told me, "was sold to get home to Dundee, Whitby, or Lyme"—all of which were famous British whaling ports.

The resemblances between the two schools of scrimshaw (which will be further discussed in a moment) have thus posed a problem for the collector. They have a further and much greater importance, however, in that here for the first time perhaps in art history we have a really international art form, one that is made simultaneously in two countries and appreciated equally in both. Only the history of ivory carving can produce strange anomalies of this sort; another will be noticed when we discuss the prisoner-of-war model ship, an artifact supposedly only made by French prisoners and yet in fact made so skillfully by American captives that their work has passed, unchallenged, as that of the French.

The motives that led to the production of scrimshaw have never been properly explored. It has been assumed, almost without question, that it was encouraged by the master to prevent Satan finding work for idle hands to do, and that was an end of it. There is no doubt that many captains did believe that scrimshaw was good to keep the men's minds off their grievances. "It was to prevent melancholia, masturbation, and madness during the very long passages" remarks Captain Spencer Johnson. A skipper faced with a really mutinous crew, however, would probably be more inclined to "haze" them and try to break

their spirit by exhausting them physically with laborious and unnecessary tasks. On the other hand, one bent on simply amusing his crew would probably turn them to "dance and skylark" or encourage them to play checkers so as to take their minds off throwing iron belaying pins at their officers, as Captain Claret does in Herman Melville's *White Jacket*.

It has also been said that the primary purpose of making scrimshaw was to produce a present that would be a token of remembrance to a sweetheart or wife back home. There is no doubt that much of the scrimshaw made can in fact be accounted for in just this way.[7] Many of the items made were household gear, clothes pegs, bodkins, wick pickers, and, of course, the familiar pastry crimp.

It is easy to associate these humble gifts with the sailor's low standard of living and fairly simple home. There are other examples of scrimshaw that were obviously intended as gifts, such as for example the corset busk. These stay busks, which measured about 14 inches in length, were sown into a pocket into the middle of a bodice. Writers about scrimshaw have said, archly, that the purpose of a stay busk was to prevent over-familiarity on the part of suitors. They may indeed have had that secondary purpose, but their primary one was to enable a girl who cared about her appearance—but did not have enough money to be fashionable or to buy her clothes—to stitch her own stays at home. They were in fact a makeover for an old or homemade pair of stays. Now a poor, but neat and respectable girl who was handy with a needle was just the sort of sweetheart a sailor would have—if he were lucky—and it is not difficult to see him patiently making her a busk

---

7. Schuyler Camman, in "Carvings In Walrus Ivory," Philadelphia University Museum Bulletin, vol. 18, no. 3, September 1954, comes near to it. "Though the whalemen generally intended these carved or engraved walrus tusks and whales' teeth for their friends and relatives at home, they often ended by bartering them in the foreign ports where their ships put in. Thus carved walrus tusks found their way to such distant places as Valparaiso, Chile, and other South American seaports."

in the foc'sle by the light of a teapot lamp full of sludge.

Not all whalermen had sweethearts, wives, friends, families, or homes. Frank Bullen, a Britisher who shipped aboard a New Bedford whaler in 1875, congratulated himself that if he were to drop overboard tomorrow, no one would be a penny the worse. Men like Bullen could have had no sentimental motive in undertaking scrimshaw. Why then did they make it? Captain Spencer Johnson supplies the answer: "It stays in your pocket (in the leather bag you have made for it) until required for currency."

Though no one has ever suspected it before, there can be little doubt that the majority of articles made in scrimshaw work were intended for sale, or as a "present" to someone in authority, such as an officer, from whom favors in return would be expected. Herman Melville, who is still our best literary source for everything to do with scrimshaw, describes just such a transaction in *White Jacket,* a novel about life on an American man o' war. The Master at Arms, a rascally officer, is dismissed from his post by the commander, Captain Claret, but the captain "because he could not bear to leave in disgrace a person who, out of the generosity of his heart, had about a year previous, presented him with a rare snuff box, fabricated from a sperm whale's tooth, with a curious silver hinge, and cunningly wrought in the shape of a whale," reinstates him.

An even more straightforward commercial transaction is recorded by Frank Bullen, a British seaman who served aboard a New Bedford whaler and who wrote about his experiences aboard her in a book that will always remain one of the great classics of the sea, *The Cruise of the "Cachalot."* "I once had an elaborate pastry cutter carved out of six whale's teeth," he recalls, "which I purchased for a pound of tobacco from a seaman in the *Coral* whaler, and afterwards sold in Dunedin, New Zealand, for £2 10/–[8],

the purchaser being decidedly of the opinion that he had a bargain.' It is a little difficult to equate prices in Australasia with those in Bullen's original home port, London, England, but at about this time the British working man was supposed on an average to spend ninepence a week on beer and baccy. So if Bullen had brought the money home with him he would have been able to keep himself in drinks and smokes for 18 months. This would surely have represented a successful commercial transaction from his point of view.

Whalemen were paid no wages, their only hope of monetary reward for their labors lying in their being present to claim the "lay" or share of the voyage, which they would get when they returned to home port. As Melville is quick to point out, many of them jumped ship (as he himself did) and in consequence never got any money at all. There were occasions when a man *had* to have money however. Supposing he fell ill in port and required the services of a doctor? American whale ships, unlike their British equivalents, carried no physicians. There were many other things he might need money for, not least of all, as Captain Spencer Jones has pointed out, to make his way home from his eventual port of landing.

Small wonder then that the whaleman used his leisure hours to manufacture what was practically a substitute currency, scrimshaw work that could be traded to a speculative shipmate for tobacco or sold for cash to a dealer in some port of call.

By 1853 when the Reverend John Wood (whom we have already met) wrote his *Illustrated Natural History,* scrimshaw had made its appearance as a regular item on the curio market in London. "In Europe," he says, "the teeth of the Cachalot or Spermaceti whale are of no great value, being considered merely as marine curiosities and often carved with rude engravings representing the chase of the animal from which they were taken, together with a very precise account of the latitude and longitude, and a tolerably accurate view of the vessel." Wood's description

___
8. Modern equivalent $6.15.

would fit any number of engraved whale's teeth in American museums, notably one in the Kynett Collection, which was made just the year before he wrote and which records the capture of a sperm whale, "by Captain M'Carty in the *Barque Adventurer,* Aug. 10, 1852, in Latitude 29° 20′ south, Longitude 34° 42′ west." Ideas of value differ, and what seemed a small sum to a rich cleric may have seemed a very large one to a poor sailor.

As a matter of fact, English people in Victoria's reign, and no doubt well-to-do folk in the colonies as well, seem to have been extremely fond of animal curios and to be prepared to pay large prices to get them. Dr. Gordon Stables, a Polar explorer writing in 1888, tells how he was accosted on a railway platform by a man who wanted to sell him some "genuine American buffalo horns." Although assured by the pedlar that they would be "quite an ornament for any gentleman's hall, sir," Stables refused to pay the very large price of five pounds.[9] Later the same evening he saw the identical horns in a friend's house. They had been sold, he reckoned, for just five times their value.

If it could be assumed that much, if not most, scrimshaw was made for sale, a lot that is puzzling, if not downright inexplicable, about the art would become clear, such as why scrimshaw artists chose to make particular kinds of carvings. The range of articles made by the scrimshoner follows close on that of the professional whalebone carver or whale ivory carver. Just as the clenched fist stick head so popular with scrimshaw artists can be paralleled by examples made by the Dieppe carvers, so some of the work turned out by professional French whalebone workers as early as 1725—parasols, fans, rods for equerries and beadles, corsets and busks, various turnery and cutler's work—does not sound so very different from what was made aboard a New Bedford whaler.

What was more, much of the commonest

kinds of scrimshaw seem very ill assorted with a seaman's cottage or lodgings. They included silkwinding swifts that would not have been out of place in a palace, ivory inlaid workboxes, inlaid writing boxes, mirror boxes, cufflinks, walking canes with ivory heads and ferules, ink stands and snuffboxes, umbrella handles, and riding whips. Sailor's wives were much more likely to wind wool on the back of a chair, or on the outstretched hands of a companion, than on elaborately constructed and beautifully carved swifts that would never have survived in a house full of children. In short, almost everything a scrimshaw artist made (with the exception of the humble, useful articles such as clothes pegs) seems to have been designed for a fairly prosperous middle-class home.

It is difficult to conceive of sailors, or their families, ever making use of some of the common types of scrimshaw—such as walking canes, for example. These were not to be found in the hands of seamen of the period—though their officers might well use them. Captain Claret is

A far-traveled art form. The patriotic American decoration on these scrimshawed whales' teeth, which includes the Stars and Stripes, Liberty, a Cat, a Mountain, an American eagle, and the Star of Liberty, did not prevent its being appreciated by a British patron, who bought it. Obviously American scrimshaw was highly thought of by British collectors. The legend on the middle tooth reads: "The General Marion of New York." The number of stars in the Stars and Stripes on the left may give a clue to the date of the piece. (Scott Polar Research Institute, Cambridge, England)

9. $12

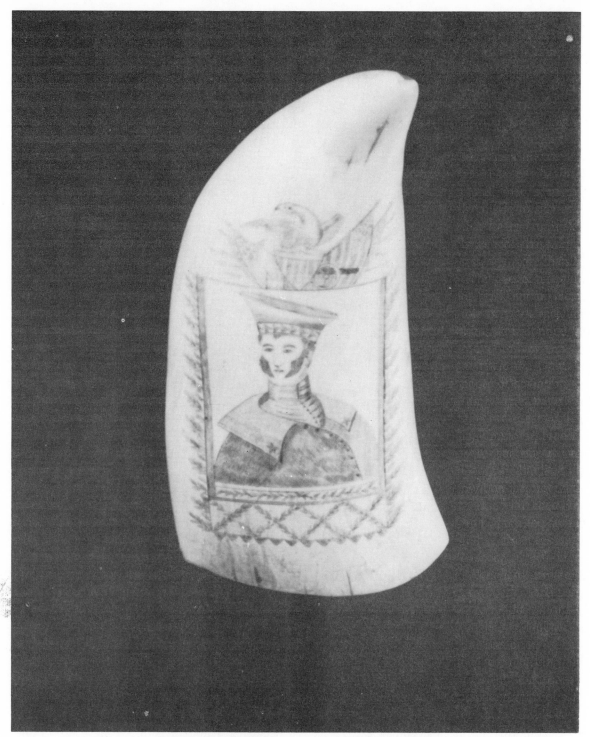

American art comes of age and secures international recognition for the first time. This flamboyantly American piece is typical of what British patrons appreciated. Note the olive branch decoration. (Dundee Museum, Scotland)

presented with a fine walking cane by his scoundrel Master at Arms. It is even more difficult to imagine a sailor using a riding whip, which reminds me of the only occasion when I ever came across a piece of scrimshaw in real life. When, as a poor student, I met the daughter of one of my professors, she was carrying a whip over which some sailor had spent many watches.

There are other reasons for supposing that a lot of the scrimshaw made was made to sell. One is that it was sometimes mass-produced. The carpenter aboard Frank Bullen's whaler started making half a dozen walking sticks at once as soon as they caught the first whale.

Unless it is assumed that much scrimshaw was made for sale it is impossible to account for the very wide distribution of pieces of purely American scrimshaw all over the world. I have been fortunate in securing illustrations of these American whale's tooth graphics from various British collections, and I could have cited examples in other British museums, such as the British Museum (Natural History) South Kensington. The pieces shown can be regarded as being American because of the subjects of their decoration. Either this shows an American ship, which is named as such, or it shows ships flying the Stars and Stripes, or it depicts whaleboats performing an operation that never took place in the Tasmanian fisheries—chasing a whale with sails set.

Although British collections are rich in American scrimshaw, it seems that those in Tasmania are richer still. Not merely is it possible to identify particular graphics as being American ones, sometimes pieces of a form identical with those in American scrimshaw collections appear, such as pastry jaggers and the like.

What is more remarkable still is the fact that American scrimshaw artists deliberately made use of foreign emblems that would make their work more salable. One fine graphic on a piece of whale jaw pan, now in the New Bedford Whaling Museum, depicts the pursuit of whales in waters east of Australia. One of the flags flown by the two vessels in the picture can be

identified as the Stars and Stripes, but the frame in which the picture is set is ornamented with a Union Jack crossed with a bordered Union flag, a Foul Anchor (a symbol of the British Admiralty), and a French Ensign, crossed with the Stars and Stripes. Finally there comes a flag that appears to be both the Stars and Stripes and the Union Jack intermingled. It would be difficult to think of any art that was more deliberately international than such a piece as this, but it is by no means unique, and I have seen scrimshawed horns incorporating both the American eagle and the British lion.

There can be no greater tribute to the art of the American scrimshaw artist than the fact that his British counterpart, when he embarked on scrimshaw, deliberately set out to copy the "New Bedford manner" and introduced into his work not merely the main themes of scrimshaw—pictures of ships, sailors, whales, and the like—but also some of the incidental ornamentation. The most important ornamental motif to be used by both sets of scrimshaw engravers is the olive branch, a device that is often unrecognizable as such because it has been given roses at the ends of the stems. This form of decoration, and the use of diced borders, which appear both on American and Tasmanian scrimshaw, testify to the success of Yankee scrimshaw in the field of international art. It was obviously regarded as a standard to which all scrimshaw work had to conform.

My argument that most scrimshaw was made for sale is, I think, quite compatible with the well-known fact that many pieces were presented by the makers to friends. Often the makers in this particular case were fairly well-to-do seafarers, captains, captains' wives, mates, and fairly literate seamen who were able to keep journals. Perhaps people of this sort did not feel the same economic urge to part with their treasures as did a whaleman who had jumped ship, had no prospect of another berth, and had no possessions except his scrimshaw work carefully treasured in the leather bag he had specially made for it.

How scrimshaw was made is a very much less

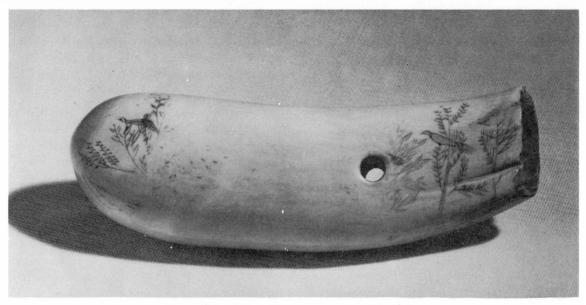

The Bird of Paradise appears on this Fiji pendant, which has been decorated by a scrimshaw artist. It is an "international" motif that can be seen on pieces of scrimshaw known to have American and British provenance. (Anthropological Museum of Aberdeen University)

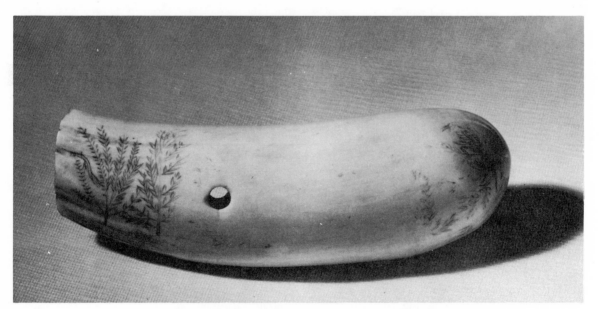

The other side of the pendant. Teeth of this sort were often used for bride-price currency. Another international motif appears that was common to American, Russian, and British ivory engravers—the olive branch. (Let us hope that this is a happy omen.) (Anthropological Museum of Aberdeen University)

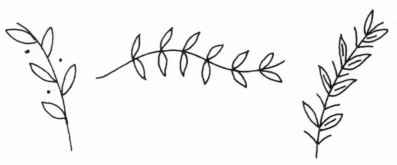

The olive branch as it appears on British scrimshaw (left), American scrimshaw, (right), and British scrimshaw again (right). See illustrations for the Russian olive branch pattern.

controversial question than why it was made. Good literary sources describe most steps in the process, and where they leave anything wanting it is possible to refer to living scrimshaw artists who were trained in the traditional methods that had no doubt been used since the art began.

Scrimshaw starts with the raw material—the lower teeth of a sperm whale or some other kind of toothed whale, such as a killer, or a piece of walrus ivory—obtained usually by trading with the Eskimos. We will disregard the other material for scrimshaw, whalebone and jawpan, because they were not ivory, though they are often spoken of as if they were, especially by Herman Melville, who, like Virgil, loves to throw a magic veil of words between the reader and the objects he describes.

There is something very primitive and archaic about the way in which the sperm teeth were hauled out of the lower jaw with a block and tackle and barreled up in brine before being set aside for the use of the crew. It is quite possible that we have here a survival of a ritual sharing out that goes back to the earliest days of whaling. One of the reasons why most masters made no difficulty about giving the men what teeth they wanted for scrimshaw was that whale's teeth contain so little ivory that they were of no commercial value, unlike, for example, walrus teeth, which were eagerly sought by 19th-century dentists because of the whiteness of the ivory. It is true that the teeth could be, and were,

used as currency on some South Sea islands, but they were a tricky medium of exchange, rather like paying for groceries in million dollar bills. On some islands teeth were considered so sacred that they could only be used as a decoration for the island temples or stored in the royal treasury. More than one war was fought because an inferior chief had got possession of a whale's tooth that, by sacred law, belonged to his superior alone.

But although it was useless to anyone else, the whale's tooth provided an admirable medium for the scrimshaw artist. The enamel on the outside of the tooth was very hard; although difficult to carve, it could be easily scratched with a nail and the hard enamel then preserved the engraving that had been made on it intact. In fact it seemed as though the scrimshaw artist had discovered something for which men had sought since the days of Ancient Egypt, indestructible pictures. On the other hand, it could be carved only with great difficulty, because there was the layer of enamel to cut through first, and once inside the tooth the carver found as good (and soft) ivory as that in an elephant's tusk.

Frank Bullen, a reluctant British seaman aboard a New Bedford whaler with a hell-driving skipper, has described the tool chest of the scrimshaw worker with some care. "The tools used are of the roughest. Some old files, softened in the fire, and filed into grooves something like saw teeth, are most used; but old knives, sail-needles, and chisels are pressed into service. The work turned out would in many cases take a very high place in an exhibition of turnery, though never a lathe was near it. Of course, a long time is taken over it, especially the polishing, which is done with oil and whiting, if it can be got, powdered pumice if it can not." Even for a modern ivory carver equipped with the best tools available it would still be a difficult task to construct some of the work that Bullen describes: "A favorite design is to carve the bone into the similitude of a rope, with 'worming' of smaller line along its lays. A handle is carved out of a whale's tooth, and insets of baleen, silver, cocoa tree, or ebony give variety and finish."

So far we have been mainly discussing carvings, not the graphics executed on whale's teeth. It is interesting to notice that the tools used for making these carvings were very like those of a modern professional ivory carver. When, for example, "Chips," the carpenter aboard the *Pequod* is about to make a new peg leg for Ahab, he exclaims: "Chisel, file, and sandpaper now!" Tools like these are still used by professional carvers.

When, however, the scrimshoner got onto graphics, he did things in a completely different way from a professional. Instead of cutting his thin, delicate lines with a graver or burin, a tool that cuts fairly deep, he used a variety of homemade tools, some fabricated for him by the cooper, but most of them adapted from the tools he used every day on the ship, such as his sail needle and jackknife. The observant Herman Melville had noticed this: "Of whales . . . in teeth," he says, "you will come across lively sketches . . . graven by the fishermen themselves on Sperm Whale teeth. . . . Some of them have little boxes of dentistical looking implements, specially intended for the skrimshandering business. But in general they toil with their jackknives alone."

Many of the American scrimshaw graphics now in English collections bear witness to the truth of Melville's remarks. Although the marks on some suggest a sail needle, which swept in and out, leaving a trough deeper at the middle than at either end, it was possible to identify, again and again, the mark of a jackknife. Either the knife had left a wedge-shaped nick in making say a dot that composed the Stars and Stripes of a flag, or a starfish-shaped nick made by twisting the point in several different directions from a central spot, or the way in which the composition was built up indicated that the tooth was held in one hand and a knife in the other.

A friend lent me a typical piece of 19th-century scrimshaw, which was a copy of a portrait of Sir Walter Raleigh. All the buttons on his doublet had been cut out in two curved sweeps. This was, of course, the simplest way of outlining them if you were using a jackknife. If, however, you had been holding a sail needle instead, it would have been much easier to go round in a circle. Another indication that a jackknife was much used for graphics is the very large number of completely straight lines that enter into many compositions. It is just as easy to make a curved line as a straight one with a sail needle, but it is much easier to make a completely straight or slightly angular line with a jackknife.

As far as I can find out, nobody attempted to examine the techniques of scrimshaw by looking at examples through a 25X magnifying glass before I began to do so. The best scrimshaw can only be fully appreciated when it is looked at through a glass of this sort. One British whaleman in Australian waters has even said outright that scrimshawers did all their work under a magnifying glass[10] and it is not difficult to see why.

Take the "Sir Walter Raleigh artist" for example. He has occasionally indulged in little sportive fancies, such as turning an ornament on a doublet in his original copy into a beautiful fish, with every scale outlined, yet only seven millimeters high. Scrimshaw—perhaps it would be better to say good scrimshaw—is very far from meriting the charges often made against

10. Quoted by W. Byden, "Scrimshaw", Hobart, Australia, 1967.

This little fish (3/10ths of an inch long) is drawn on such a small scale that it is impossible to see its construction except under a 25X magnifying glass. The fin is invisible to the naked eye. Note the starfish-shaped dot (made by twisting the point of a jackknife) that serves for the eye.

it that it is rough, crude, and lacking in artistic feeling. A piece of scrimshaw worth the name is a work of the utmost delicacy of feeling. One can see myriads of little lines, all very close together and all forming a composite pattern, but it is almost impossible to conceive how the artist had the patience, and the manual dexterity, to engrave them as they lie.

This discussion of how scrimshaw was made might well end with the descriptions given of how modern work was carried out, and is still made by genuine scrimshoners, not fakers but seafarers who are worthy descendants of those Michelangelos of the sludge lamp whose work we have just been discussing. Captain C. E. Parkes, who was in close touch with scrimshaw in his seagoing career, has been good enough to describe for me one method as he remembers it.

"Regarding your inquiry about Sperm Whale's teeth, or 'Scrimshawck.' These had first to be sandpapered as they were very rough, then polished properly. Then a piece of transparent paper was placed over the tooth; then a cutting from some paper, magazine, or book was placed over the transparent paper; then numerous pricks with a pin were used to take in all of the illustration in minute holes on the tooth. Then India ink was used to fill in all the holes after they had been minutely scratched, then when the ink was quite dry, another gentle polish was given to the tooth." Captain Parkes' account gives a good idea of the step-by-step approach of the scrimshoner—first one process, then another following it, with every new direction given to the

work well thought out beforehand, nothing hurried, nothing scamped. Although Captain Parkes does not indicate what polish was used, sailmaker's wax was often used for this purpose.

Captain Spencer Johnson, whose home port is Whitby, the base for many British whalers during the 19th century, gives another invaluable account of how the craft was carried on while it was still at its peak.

"My father (a Cape Horner) taught me scrimshaw over 50 years ago. As far as I am concerned, this is how it goes. Two to four months to get used to the Tooth (Sperm) less for a Killer (whale) in your pocket the whole time, daily work on and off watch on deck, because of the smell when scraping and polishing with china clay and whale oil. The hands became quite soft and female-like, 'Homeward Bound.'

"One day to complete the Scrimshaw, fine weather, N. of 45, a good needle, and a pad of lampblack and a *peaceful mind* (happy ship) Then to make the leather bag and it stays in your pocket until required for currency.

"To me there is only one way, as described, and that is too long for today, passages are too short. I still use this method, and one tooth George (Commander Naish) saw took three months of very hard work and two days of scrimshaw."

Captain Spencer Johnson's technique, it will be noticed, differs substantially from that of Captain Parkes. For one thing, he makes no mention of using a tracing or paste down as the blueprint for his engraving; for another he uses lampblack instead of india ink. No doubt at every stage of the art different methods were in use.

It would be premature to try to arrange different types of scrimshaw into the periods at which they were made at this stage of our knowledge. After all, the discovery of the Hull boxes has pushed back the earliest known pieces by just 266 years, and there must be a lot of undiscovered country lying in between. Certain general remarks about the dating of any piece of scrimshaw, however, may be made.

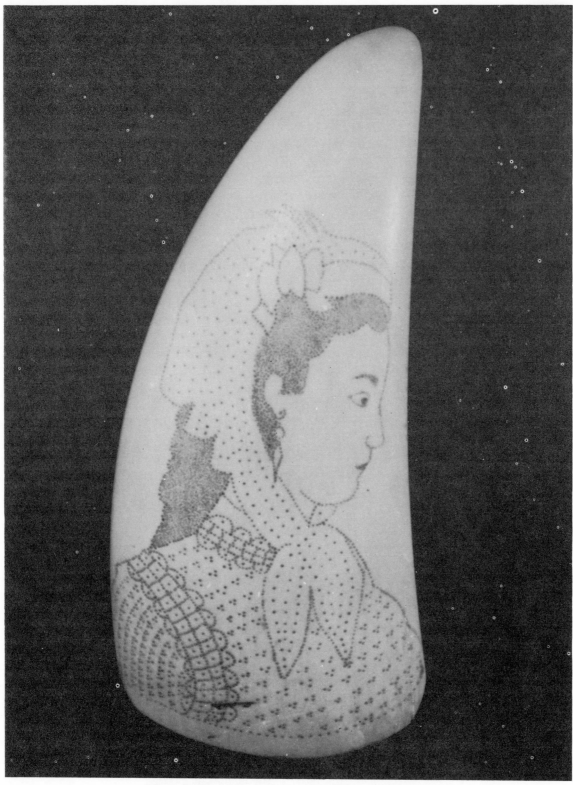

More than one method of making scrimshaw was in use. Here (as Captain Parkes has described) a design has been laboriously pricked through the paper pattern with a sail needle, a manner of operation that recalls tattooing. (Dundee Museum, Scotland)

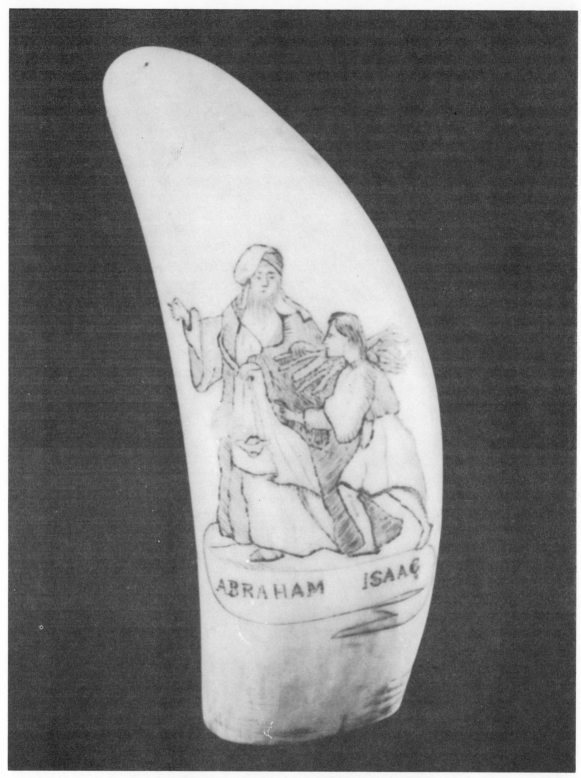

A variation on the page 55 method. The prick
marks are still evident but they have been joined
to form lines; scratches have been added to build
up the pattern. (Dundee Museum, Scotland)

Owing to the over hunting of the sperm whale, few whales live to achieve a great age and the size of their teeth is consequently much less than that of the contemporaries of Moby Dick. The average whale tooth that can be bought in an ivory warehouse in London, such as Natural Products in the Minories, is only six ounces. Consequently, a piece of scrimshaw executed on a very large tooth is much more likely than not to be genuine. Size is not an infallible test of the authenticity of a whale tooth graphic. Teeth were brought back that were scraped up, polished, but never engraved. These could be utilized for a much later carving. I bought one in the Rows in Chester that weighed 12 ounces, and quite recently Miss M. Joyce Bidder showed me one she had just bought that was nine inches long, only a few inches short of the world record.

A genuine piece of scrimshaw has often aged to a mellow, golden hue. This is because it was polished with oil, which makes ivory yellow, and because many teeth were intended as mantlepiece ornaments. This is why they often have a double groove cut round the base, where they have been sawed across the hollow part. The heat and the draft of their position just over the fire would help to darken them. On the other hand, teeth that have been coated with some yellow-colored varnish to give them an "aged" look should be distrusted, even though their condition may be the result of misuse by some former owner rather than deliberate faking.

A really old piece of scrimshaw ought to have plenty of accidental scratches on it, as it has probably been knocked about a bit in the course of its long life. It should also bear marks that can be identified with *some* of the tools we know were used for scrimshaw—jackknife, sail needle, file, saw, and sharkskin or sandpaper. A saw leaves parallel lines across a piece of ivory that are much deeper than the lines made by a file, which are also parallel. The Sir Walter Raleigh scrimshawed tooth that I have described has been unmistakably trimmed off with a saw. Look closely at the tool marks on a piece of scrimshaw through a 25X magnifying glass. If the cuts go very deep, distrust them, they may have been made with a modern burin or graver. Use a sail needle and jackknife on a whale's tooth and compare the marks with those on any piece of scrimshaw you are examining.

The color of ink used on a piece of scrimshaw may give you a clue to its age. Although india ink and red ink have been with us for a very long time, blue ink is supposed to have been introduced by the British firm of Stephens at the start of the 19th century.

Just because a piece of scrimshaw is modern there is no need to suppose that it is necessarily a fake. Scrimshaw continued to be made on British whalers, such as those owned by Salveson of Leith, by the mixed Scottish and Norwegian crews until well into living memory. The last European whaler made her final trip only two years ago.

Chapter 3.

American Ivory Carving: The Prisoner Model

Toward the end of the great French war excited crowds of English rustics in smock frocks and corduroys gathered on the roads leading to Dartmoor, agog to catch sight of the first batch of American prisoners, captured in the War of 1812, which was being marched to the prison camp that already housed so many French captives. The Devonshire yokels knew of only one kind of American, the Red Indians, in war paint and scalp lock, who brandished their hatchets and did their war dance before excited audiences at the side shows of fairs. Here was an occasion to feast their eyes, for nothing, upon a spectacle of which they would normally have but a brief, expensive glimpse.

At last the weary column wound into sight and the watching throng caught their first glimpse of the men in dust-stained uniforms or Ordnance Department slops that were issued to prisoners. More significant than the looks of defiance that the prisoners cast at the crowd was the forest of bayonets of the guards who closed the line of march. The British government had found by experience that, although two or three militiamen were enough to escort hundreds of French prisoners over the whole breadth of the land, American prisoners needed a guard per man, otherwise they would inevitably escape. A big sigh of disappointment went up from the waiting yokels. "Why, they be no more savages

than we are!" said one of them in disgust.

Prison life for captives of the wars was nothing new in England. It was just another of those scourges for mankind thought up by Napoleon. Britain had been willing to exchange all her French prisoners for English ones on a man-for-man basis. Napoleon had refused. He wanted four Frenchmen for every one Englishman he released. Though he was never tired of talking about the cruelty of the English in shutting up their prisoners on the Hulks (floating battleships that were used to house refractory prisoners) and in prison camps like Dartmoor and Norman's Cross, he never gave his agreement to an exchange on equal terms, which would have meant that they were all released. Release for the French prisoners only came when he himself went off to a much more comfortable prison, first on Elba, then on St. Helena.

It was only the patriotic Frenchmen who elected to stay in British prisons. True sons of the Revolution, they went on singing *Ça Ira* (the revolutionary hymn) in their captivity long after Frenchmen on the other side of the channel had forgotten all about the Revolution and its ideals. Napoleon's other soldiers, the unwilling conscripts from the satellite countries, were only too glad to enlist in what was still technically an American regiment, though in British service, the 60th Royal Americans. This corps, formerly known as "The Loyal American Provincials," had been originally formed from German and Swiss Protestants who had settled in America, but it had now become a sort of British Foreign Legion—a Tower of Babel with muskets.

Because it was much easier to catch a Frenchman on sea than on land, many of the prisoners in England were seamen; in fact the first arrivals at Norman's Cross were *matelots* from the *Revolutionnaire* that had been captured by the *Saucy Arethusa*. George Borrow, whose father was a militiaman guarding the prisoners at this big depot, remarked that Norman's Cross was a cross to many a Norman. There must have been many sailors from France's principal maritime province in the prison, and probably many of them were from Dieppe, which as will be seen in the next chapter was the center of French ivory carving.

It is to this sprinkling of professional ivory carvers, conscripted into Napoleon's navy and captured by the Royal Navy, that we owe the prisoner-of-war model in ivory, or ivory and bone, an art form that was begun by the French prisoners and continued by their American successors. Because the American ivory carvers were going to inherit not merely the methods but the actual tools and stock in trade of raw material (as well as the good will of their fellow inmates) when the French prisoners left England following the first fall of Napoleon, it is necessary to look rather closely at French prisoner models if we are to appreciate the American ones properly.

The question of whether Dieppe carvers were really responsible for the upsurge of ivory and bone carving in British prisons has aroused a good deal of controversy ever since Commander Naish's aunt, writing under the initials "F.C.P.N." in the *Mariner's Mirror*[1] first established the connection between the free and the imprisoned carvers. As Jane Toller, the most recent writer on prisoner-of-war crafts, has pointed out, prisoner carving in ivory and bone is much too

skillful to suggest anything except a professional carver. It would have been too much of a coincidence if the ivory ship model, a favorite outlet for the Dieppe carver since the late 18th century, and the identical ivory ship model of the British prison had evolved independently. That the two sets of models stem from an identical source can be seen from a comparison between existing prisoner models and a model that we know to have been made in Dieppe, such as the *Ville de Dieppe,* presented in 1811 by the Dieppe ivory carvers to Napoleon's Empress, Marie Louise. Apart from the principal similarity, the technique used to work the ivory, and the way it is developed for sails and rigging, there are other minor resemblances between prisoner models and ones known to have been made across the Channel. They include the making up of the base for the model from a marquetry of exotic woods, with an ornamental railing round the ship. The considerable use of bone on many of the prisoner models which, like scrimshaw, are often a composite creation of ivory and bone, is another indication of Dieppe craftsmanship. The natural inclination of a prisoner would have been to eat the bones he found in his food.

Yankee inmates of the camps devised an ingenious means of preparing these bones into a nourishing jelly, and no doubt they shared the secret with their French companions. The Dieppe carvers, however, had been making use of a lot of bone in their ivory work since before the Revolution. It helped to eke out the ivory, which was expensive stuff, and did just as well in some parts of a carving that are normally little seen, such as the bottom strakes of an ivory ship .for example. "I visited an ivory carver," noted Bernardin de St. Pierre in 1782 while he was staying at Dieppe. "A man of taste called Le Flaman. In a corner of his shop there was a great pile of beef bones. This is the most solid of all bones; it gets yellow less quickly than ivory." The same author also mentions horse and sheep bones being used for carving. The note of minuteness and delicacy of finish, which are so obvious in many prisoner ships where the tiniest details of

---

1. *Mariner's Mirror,* 1921, 89.

the ship, such as the carriages of the guns, are covered with delicate miniature carving, are also characteristic of Dieppe. These features are shown in other prisoner models besides those made of ships, such as the domino sets that pack into a tiny wooden shoe. These are very like the minute games of skittles made in Dieppe later in the century, in which all the skittles stow away into a tiny round box turned out of ivory.

The conclusive argument for a connection between Dieppe and the British prison camps, however, is that after 1815 Dieppe carvers who had been imprisoned in the Hulks (no doubt for trying to escape) made models of the derelict wooden line of battleships that had been their prisons. These models remain in Dieppe. "The Hulks were then quite fresh," says Michel Belloncle, "in the memory of the people who had made them, and who had been kept prisoners in them."

Of course not every ivory ship modeler came from Dieppe; one of the most famous, a certain Garnier, was from St. Malo. But there was one skilled modeler who bore a name connected with Dieppe—Germain Lamy, the same surname that appears on the flyleaf of the account of the ivory country written by the Dieppe explorer Chambonneau, which will be referred to in the next chapter. In 1811 Lamy was building his model ships at Forton, which was to become famous as a center for American model making. The average maker of ivory ships was anonymous, however, in fact he was part of a team, each engaged in making a different part of the ivory ship. Team work had a lot to do with the very finished look of the model ships, and also accounts for the fact that there seem to be so many of them. "From the great number of these bone ship models in existence," writes an authority, "perhaps some will think that the Dieppe tradesmen-seamen must have been very industrious." She goes on to point out that between 1793 and 1815, 60,147 Frenchmen were captured from privateers alone, not counting prisoners from ships of the French navy, and adds: "There must have been among them a fair pro-

portion of Dieppe men, with a knowledge of ivory working, men who had been conscripted or who had embarked in privateers owing to slackness of trade."

Not everyone in a prison camp became a ship modeler, and it depended largely on your social level in the prison whether you took to ivory carving or not. Amongst these expatriated citizens of the land of liberty, equality, and fraternity, the most rigid caste barriers soon began to arise. At the top of the social scale were the "lords," lucky individuals who were sent remittances of money from home. Then at the bottom were the "Romans," men who had reverted to the status of social outcasts. They had gambled away not merely their clothes, but the daily ration that stood between them and starvation. In between this top and bottom class stood the "laboureurs," prisoners who were determined to make the best of their captivity by using their enforced leisure to produce luxury goods for the English leisured class, who, it will be remembered, were cut off from the *articles de Paris* by the British blockade. Dartmoor, Norman's Cross, and the other prison camps became a sort of Dieppe and Paris on British soil producing artistic frivolities of a high order that were eagerly bought by the British. Far from taking advantage of the poor prisoners, visitors to the camp and dealers who bought their wares seem to have treated them very fairly. Germain Lamy went so far as to declare that he had never had anything to complain of about the conduct of his English customers. The French were compelled to concentrate on ivory and bone carvings and just a few other crafts, such as paper folding and straw mosaic, because English craftsmen refused to allow them to produce anything that might compete with British goods. Straw plaiting, which was beautifully made by the prisoners, was seized by the guards during armed raids on their quarters and burned in a bonfire, while the despoiled prisoners shouted execrations, mixed with cries of "Vive l'Empereur!" from their barrack windows. Another incentive for prisoners to concentrate on making ivory and bone toys was that

French prisoner model of a 74-gun ship. Where
bone is used in conjunction with ivory (as here),
the former can be distinguished by the black
hair lines running through it. (Science Museum,
London)

the rewards could be very great. Although few if any of the prisoners at Portchester Castle had had any experience of craftsmanship before they saw England, says a French captive, St. Aubin, this did not prevent many of them returning home "with full pockets." The same story is told by the Reverend Robert Forby, who visited Norman's Cross in June, 1807. "We walked to see the barracks for French prisoners," he noted. "Their dexterity in little handicraft and nicknacks, particularly in making toys of the bones of their meals, will put many pounds into the pockets of several of them. We were very credibly assured that there are some who will carry away with them £200 or £300."[2] Compared with the free but impoverished farm laborers outside the camps, the prisoners seemed "very rich" to contemporaries.

Although the prisoners made all sorts of models—including obscene ones, with which the poet Southey complained, "every pedlar's pack is filled," and some of them, such as the models of guillotines, theatres, trial scenes, and the prison camps themselves are beautifully contrived—the favorites were, and have remained, the model ships. Sometimes these models were made completely of ivory. (Commander Naish owns a very fine example, but prisoner models were rather like an Irish stew: anything that would serve its turn was used.) When the craftsmen could not get hold of enough ivory, they used bone, whalebone, or wood. When they could not get pieces of ivory of sufficient length to make rigging, they used human hair, literally creating their artistic work out of their own heads, as it were. Of course they could buy as much ivory as they wanted in the prison market; they could even buy gold if they were goldsmiths, but obviously demand sometimes exceeded supply. Sometimes a patron who wanted a model made in some specially exotic material would supply the raw material himself. Archdeacon Strong, a frequent visitor to Norman's

Cross and a good patron of the prisoners' work, provided mahogany for a model that he wanted to be made of the block house in the camp.

Bone is at best an unsatisfactory substitute for ivory, if there is any carving to be done to it. It is much less flexible than ivory, much harder, and much more brittle and likely to break. The only nicknacks that my faithful char lady has been able to break, after years of dusting, is a Chinese bone cricket cage. Moreover, bone never looks as well as ivory because of the unsightly black lines that streak it here and there.

Just because of these lines, and also because bone is whiter, it can be distinguished from ivory, which is much yellower and softer looking, and which often shows "striation" lines of creamy white alternating with rather darker yellow. The differences between ivory and bone can usually be seen on a model composed of both of them. In a model such as "Ocean" in the Science Museum, London, the ornamental balustrades by the entry ports, the railing of the quarter deck, the ship's boats, and other decorative parts of the vessel are made from ivory, which is much easier to carve. The plain and undecorated parts of the ship, such as the spars or the planking, are made from bone.

Although it took some time for the Americans to adjust to prison life, because they were kept separate from the French at first and because of the difficulty of guarding the two nationalities when they were mixed together, and although they were sometimes debarred from the prison market for a time, as at Dartmoor, eventually they were granted the privileges of visiting the French and of trading. Some of the prisoners were so pleased at this concession that they hung out banners announcing that at last they had got what they had been fighting the war for: "Free Trade And Seamens' Rights." Before long the prisoners had shaken down into orderly, disciplined communities. The Americans were impressed by the way in which the more respectable and decent Frenchmen had organized their lives. The French community on Dartmoor was in some ways like a little French town; it had

---

2. At modern rate of exchange about $738.

Details such as the stern galleries of this French prisoner model of the 120-gun ship *Ocean* could be much more readily carved in ivory than in brittle bone. (Science Museum, London)

schools, shops, a church, a theatre—everything, as one Frenchman bitterly remarked, just as it was in France, except that there were no women! Like the French the Americans soon isolated and disciplined the more rowdy element in their midst, and at Dartmoor a self-elected chief called "Black Dick" kept control over the ne'er-do-wells in the prison.

If there was one thing that must have impressed the Americans, it was the French ivory and bone models. In the secluded and cloistered conditions of the prisons the Dieppe carvers had been able to bring their art to a pitch it had never reached since classical times. In particular they had revived an art form of which nothing seems to have been heard since the days of the Roman Empire, the ultra miniature ship model. The Roman writer Pliny had described one of these. It was so small that it could be covered by the outstretched wings of a fly, yet it was a complete ship in every part. Compare this model with one made by the St. Malo carver Garnier. It was a tiny vessel two inches long, with every part worked exactly to scale. The microscopic brass guns could be run out, and the yards lowered by running tackle made from human hair. Garnier had taken a year to build this model and he sold it for $246.

The price that a good ivory or bone ship model would fetch was often more than an ordinary seaman had ever possessed in his life, or even hoped to acquire. One of Lamy's ships, which he built with the help of a shipmate in six months' time, sold for £40. Another ship of the line, made by the prisoners of Portchester Castle, was a foot long and fetched $611. Many Americans, on being shown these models by their French fellow prisoners, and being told what they would fetch, must have become suddenly possessed with the idea that they too could become modelers and carvers, and perhaps buy themselves a farm with the proceeds of their handiwork. The more adventurous among them probably felt that if they could only acquire enough guineas, they might be able to bribe their guards and escape. Escape was never far away from the thoughts of

most of the prisoners, many of whom spent long hours trying to tunnel out of the compound. One prisoner among the many thousands illustrates the longing for home that haunted them all. A pilot from Philadelphia, he had left his house in the early hours of the morning telling his wife that he would be home for breakfast—all he had to do was to take a ship out of the harbor. Unfortunately he piloted the outward bound craft under the guns of a waiting British naval vessel, and for the rest of the war he was left to speculate as to what he would have had for breakfast.

Sometimes escape and artistry went hand in hand, as with a group of prisoners who painstakingly made themselves British uniforms and equipment, correct in every detail down to the bayonets on the muskets, which were made from cardboard covered with silver paper, then fell in behind the guard as it was being relieved, and marched off into the foggy Devon evening.

There is a strong competitive element in New Englanders, who must have composed many of the seamen prisoners, and probably one of the English guards pointed to a ship model and scornfully told an American that the French were much cleverer than his fellow countrymen. That was enough; the Americans took lessons from their French fellow prisoners, probably paying for their tuition with the allowance of money for soap and coffee of one and a half cents, later raised to two a day, which the United States Government agent paid them. Some prisoners had earned prize money while serving as unwilling pressed men in the British navy, others got remittances from home. With this money they were able to acquire the necessary stock in trade and tools and equipment. All seem to have been hard workers, although they respected the Sabbath and did not work on Sunday, unlike the French. Many of them may have carved ivory before while working scrimshaw in the whaling fleets. Some of the prisoners were obviously men of high artistic ability, only life in a foc'sle or on a farm had so far not allowed them to discover that they had it. One American prisoner became so adept at making woodcarvings in the Chinese manner that his handiwork sold for large sums in Plymouth and Moretonhampstead and he was able to live in prison in comparative comfort. Those Americans who were seamen had probably spent much more time at sea than the French. Service in the French navy, or in a French privateer, tended to take the form of a one-way voyage. Very few French ships stayed at sea for long (they were captured by the British cruisers), in fact the only French ship of the line about which Napoleon had no fears was the ivory three-decker that the ivory carvers of Dieppe had presented to Marie Louise. Their first-hand experience of ship construction must have been an invaluable asset to the American prisoners when it came to constructing model ships. One of the criticisms often made of French prisoner models is that some of them were constructed by people who had no practical knowledge of seamanship. Lastly, the Americans possessed the advantage of talking English, and the kind of English that would be more readily understood in any part of Britain than that spoken by British people from different parts of the country. This must have helped them a good deal in their discussions with dealers and patrons.

The Americans soon made as much progress in carving in a few months as the Dieppe ivory workers had made in 400 years, so that their models have passed, undistinguished, into the body of prisoner ship models. Although these models vary somewhat in quality, the best of them have always been hailed as some of the finest carvings ever made. They were eagerly bought by connoisseurs at the time, and they command enormous and steadily rising prices today.

No one has ever tried to sort out the American model ships from the French ones, though R. Morton Nance suggested that perhaps American frigate models would be better than their battleships, as there were no United States ships of the line. However many American prisoners served, as we have seen, as impressed men on British three deckers, while about 30 of them had served on ships of the French navy.

It is now time that we observed an American carving team at work. They are two seamen, neither of whom has done any craftwork before his imprisonment, and both of whom would have been puzzled to drill a hole or file two pieces of metal to a close joint if they had been set such a task while at liberty. They have been spending weeks building a miniature three-decker, using as raw material bones from the cookhouse, which they have sawn into thin slabs three-sixteenths of an inch wide, scraped to a high polish, and used to plank up the decks and sides of the model ship. If enough bones were not available from the cookhouse, they bought the bones that their comrades had saved from their meals. The planks on the three-decker are so accurately fastened to the sides of the ship with brass pins that the finished hull is as smooth as though it had been made from a single piece. The team of carvers began with no tools but a knife and a needle (the tools of the scrimshaw artist), but by dint of selling their allowance of meat for a penny, they have gradually added to their workshop a file, a pair of pliers, a small saw, a little glue, a few skeins of silk for the cordage, brass wire for the pinnings, and a coarser wire for the guns. The model, which is now completed, has each gun bored and mounted upon running carriages, complete with tackle, a movable capstan, wheel, and rudder. Each block is sheaved through the rigging and there is a full complement of boats and anchors. The most experienced seaman in the prison cannot detect a rope out of place, or anything in the model that is not perfectly to scale.

This account, which is taken from an anonymous American prisoner, who calls himself "The Greenhorn," suggests that perhaps American models were nearer to an actual ship and less fanciful and highly decorative than the French ones. It would, after all, be much easier for an American to learn modeling than carving. When we come across a model in which every part of the ship is covered with ornamental carving, in unusual and even uncomfortable places, such as the thwarts of a ship's boat, it may be French

Ship model made by American prisoners at Dartmoor Prison, 1812–1815, given to the East Indian Marine Society by Commodore Bainbridge, USN, 1822. This model does not show the American ivory carver at his best, but it is something to be able to point to any model ship and say it is American. All the others made by American prisoners were acquired by English collectors shortly after they were constructed, and have now merged indistinguishably in the body of "prisoner models" that British collectors regard as all French. (Courtesy The Peabody Museum of Salem)

rather than American.

From whatever school they emerged, whether it was American or French, prisoner models ought not to be judged solely on their accuracy. To condemn an ivory ship because it is carrying too many spars or the wrong number of guns is rather like condemning the Winged Victory of Samothrace because the figure of the Victory is too large for the bows of the trireme upon which she stands. It was almost impossible to construct a completely accurate model in such an intractable material as bone, and even when ivory is used it is often impracticable to make up a ship's boat in ivory planking instead of simply carving it from a block of ivory. Obvious departures from accuracy, such as the arrangement of plaques of ivory or bone to form the sides of the hull or the use of figureheads whose arms are pegged to their body, show that complete accuracy was never intended. The nature of the models themselves shows that they were not serious scale models, such as dockyard models that were used as blueprints for great ships, but rather toys for grownup children. Hence their working gear consisted of guns that could be run in and out, yards that could be raised and lowered, and so forth.

In some ways the Masters of the Model Ship found more appreciative patrons in England than they would have in their native France. The average Frenchman is probably repelled by anything childish in a work of art, the average Englishman attracted by it. Even in adult life the Duke of Wellington liked playing bears with children, but there is no record of Napoleon ever playing with the model ships the Dieppois presented to him.

Chapter 4.

Ivory Carving in France and Belgium

France

In contrast to their colleagues on the other side of the Channel who were busily engaged in making ship models for rich English milords, the ivory carvers of Dieppe began the 19th century in a mood of despondency. Trade was bad. For the Dieppois this was one of a series of ups and downs that had been going on since the 14th century when explorers from the little Norman fishing port had set out to found a settlement in Senegal, called "Little Dieppe," which was later to develop into France's principal African colony on the "Island of Ivory" in the Senegal river.

Because, as we have seen, an Anglo-Dutch fleet had razed Dieppe to the ground in 1694, "We note with distress," wrote the town historian, Michel Hardy, "the almost complete absence of historical documents about our ancient Dieppe ivory carvers." Some years ago I was able to discover two treatises by the 17th-century French explorer and administrator Louis Moreau de Chambonneau,[1] which at least threw a little

---

1. The full French text of Chambonneau's two treatises, with my introduction and notes, appear in the *Bulletin de l'Institut Fondamental d'Afrique Noire,* Dakar, Tome xxx, Série B, No. 1, janvier, 1968. A translation of part of the text into English is published in *African Studies,* volume 26, no. 2., 1967. Witwatersrand University Press.

light on how the Dieppe ivory workers got their raw material.

By 1674 Chambonneau explained to his readers there were very few elephants left near to the Settlement (the present city of St. Louis in Senegal). One had to go 80 leagues (about 240 miles) up river to see them roaming the jungle, and at least 150 leagues to be able to effect a trade in ivory in considerable quantities. Chambonneau described how three or four villages of the Senegalese would unite to hunt elephants and kill them with spears and arrows, so as to enjoy a feast.

"I found their flesh rather tough," Chambonneau confesses, "but how could it be otherwise seeing that some elephants live for 200 years?" Although Chambonneau was a traveler and proconsul rather than a sculptor, he was a thorough Dieppois in that he knew all about ivory. "The set of teeth of the hippopotamus," he remarks, "is very suitable for making carvings, and its ivory is much finer than that of the elephant."

There can be no doubt that although the Dieppois were the most esteemed ivory carvers in Europe, they were finding it difficult to make ends meet. "These costly products," wrote another Dieppe historian, Abbé Guibert, in 1740, "have had a chequered career. There are still some shops where one can find good workmanship, but the small outlet for sales, and consequently the modest amount of the workman's reward, makes it difficult to obtain skilled craftsmen. They are becoming scarcer and, in spite of that, they do not become any better paid."

Bad though things were, the abolition of God and the Aristocracy by the French Revolution made them a lot worse. The Dieppe carvers had filled every church in France with holy water stoups, crucifixes, descents from the cross, paxes, and the like, most of them of very high quality, unlike the rather stereotyped religious art of the 19th century. They had also worked hard to satisfy noble lay patrons for whom they had made fans, *bonbonnières,* vases, snuff graters, jewelery, perfume flasks, ornaments for the table, and particularly *navettes.*

The *navette,* an article not known in contemporary America or England, was a spindle on which the silks for embroidery were wound. It was a sort of symbol of the fine lady of the period, just as the dress sword was that of the fine gentleman. But with the advent of the Revolution those fine ladies who had not been able to emigrate dropped their *navettes* hastily and took to carrying shopping baskets so as to pass themselves off as *femmes du peuple.* It had become a crime to appear to be idle, and overnight Dieppe found its market gone.

Ivory ship presented by the Town of Dieppe to Marie Louise, accompanied by the words: "May your life never encounter more storms than does this vessel, Madam."

By 1791 the eight shopkeepers, two ivory carvers, and six ivory sculptors who had supplied the trade were ruined. Nobody dared as much as order an ivory needle case or darning egg for a *corbeil de mariage*. In despair the craftsmen began making purely utilitarian objects, such as toys, by the dozen. A few tried to capitalize on contemporary patriotic feeling by producing scenes of military life, bas reliefs of members of the Grand Army saving their comrades in battle, and the like, but these were not successful, either from the artistic or commercial point of view. So sculptors, unable to make a living in Dieppe, left for Paris and Rouen.

In an attempt to give the town's industry a fillip, Napoleon visited Dieppe in 1802, accompanied by Josephine. The Empress was presented with a model of a 74-gun ship by the girls of the village, one of whom made her a pretty speech, saying that they hoped her life would be as free from storms as the ship would be. Almost the same speech and present were to serve for Marie Louise a few years later. The present was a significant one, showing that the ship model was one of the most popular outlets for the Dieppe carver. When Napoleon returned in 1810 he ordered another ship from Belletete, who delivered it himself at the Louvre and was given a rouleau of gold napoleons as payment.

Contemporary Dieppe ivory carver, M. Jean Colette, at work on a ship model.

Napoleon also bought two medals showing Minorca, at 80 livres each; a snuffbox decorated with a scene of one vessel pursuing another, at the same price; a scent bottle for 15 livres; and a *bonbonnière*, representing Susanna in the bath, for 40 livres. These purchases probably represented the emperor's desire to stimulate trade rather than his artistic admiration. When he really liked something in the way of art, such as the great collection owned by his brother-in-law, Prince Borghese, he usually took it without payment. On the other hand he was very sensitive to criticism of the economy. Madame Junot tells us he used to wander round the shops of Paris in disguise, enquiring what trade was like. When told by one lapidary that the emperor's wars were killing business, he sent a footman from the palace to purchase two very expensive vases. None of the Dieppe carvers was given commissions to make presents for foreign princes, and Napoleon's own most expensive outlay on an ivory carving seems to have been a wonderful Chinese temple model, which he bought in the Indies as a present for Josephine and which was captured by a British cruiser. Although the chivalrous British government offered to return the Empress' present after the Peace of Amiens, Napoleon haughtily refused. He was not going to allow *perfide Albion* to appear in a good light, even though it meant depriving his wife of a plaything in which she would have delighted.

Refused substantial help from the Emperor, the Dieppe carvers waited for better times, concentrating meanwhile on the production of marine motifs, which seem to have become very popular in France at this time, possibly because the French were beginning to have a nostalgic yearning for the sea travel denied them by the British blockade.

The municipality set up a school of design in Dieppe under Marie Joseph Flouest, a painter who had begun life as an ivory carver, carving fan leaves at 20 livres a leaf. This school was going to do some very good work in forming the style of some of the best carvers of the century, such as P. A. Graillon.

Fan in carved and gilt ivory, painted by E. Moreau. Shown at the Paris Exhibition of 1867. Marie Joseph Flouest, the instructor at the Dieppe Craft school, began life by carving fans like this at 20 livres a leaf. (Victoria and Albert Museum, London)

The better times for which the Dieppois had been hoping came suddenly with the fall of the Empire and the return of the Bourbons. The carvers swept their busts of Marie Louise and the King of Rome, their Napoleonic eagles and bees under the counter, and renamed their ship models with good royalist names, such as *Henri Quatre*. They embraced their relatives who had now returned from British prison camps, their pockets jingling with the guineas that they had earned selling ship models, and prepared to welcome the first British tourists. These were not long in arriving in the shape of the army of occupation, which was quartered in France after the downfall of Napoleon. Besides the English, it included Russians, who were also good customers of the Dieppe craftsmen.

On the heels of the military came the first civilian tourists France had seen for 13 years. The English visitors had decided that life was a lot cheaper in France than in England, while Dieppe was nearer to London than many English watering places. Some of the visitors to France, such as Beau Brummell, had come because they had contracted debts in England and had to live abroad where they were safe from arrest. Brighton had just risen to eminence as the most fashionable English holiday resort, and you could sail directly from Brighton to Dieppe. English people had been fond of Dieppe ivories in the 18th century, so much at least one may infer from a picture by Joseph Vernet, showing the port in 1765. A pedlar waits for English visitors to disembark on the quay, he has a basket slung in front of him, full of little *articles de Dieppe,* and even has a large crucifix hanging round his neck.

The English visitors to Dieppe brought with them an unheard-of novelty: sea bathing. Napoleon had discouraged people from bathing during the Empire; he felt too strongly the proximity of the English blockading fleets. After their first astonishment was over, French holiday-makers followed the English tourists into the water, and also copied the English habit of buying ivories after their bath.

The future of the ivory carving industry became assured when there arrived, as a regular summer visitor to the little town, a beautiful princess, the Duchesse de Berry. Caroline Ferdinande Louise was the daughter of the King of Naples, whose dynasty had always patronized the arts. She was also the widow of the heir to the French throne, the Duke de Berry, who had been assassinated by a republican fanatic while escorting her from the opera house. Caroline had given birth to the "miracle baby," who would in turn claim the throne of France after her husband's death, and it is no wonder that French society began to flock to Dieppe from the moment of her first visit there in 1823.

So many visitors now came to Dieppe for the summer that the grateful municipality built a theatre, so that the Duchesse could satisfy her passion for the drama, while the ivory carvers, to whom she was a magnificent patron, presented her with a *toilette* in which the Arts and Sciences, allegorized by children, supported her coat of arms, quartered with that of the town. The whole design was surrounded with a wreath of ivy, symbol of loyal attachment. The ivory carvers as a whole now began to adopt loyal motifs for their work. Nothing was to be seen on snuffboxes but Louis XVI saying farewell to his

Nineteenth century Dieppe realism in the manner of Pierre Graillon. A group of fishers in the picturesque costume of La Polette, Dieppe's seafaring quarter, listen to a yarn while net mending goes on. Note the rendering of the sky, which is effected by minute, yet perfectly regular strokes of the scorper.

family, or the portrait of the Duchesse de Lambade.

The Duchesse was a regular sea bather, so wooden baths were built (which appear in some of the ivory carvings) to accommodate bathers. Dieppe became famous as the seaside resort of France. "During the months of summer and autumn," wrote an observer in 1848, "Dieppe is, nowadays, a Paris in miniature, with elegant shops, plays, balls, evening entertainments, and the most splendid fashions just as in the capital."

Nineteenth-century carving showing a group of
figures in local costume. (Dieppe Museum,
Dieppe, France)

Nineteenth-century carving showing a fisherman
and his son in the dress of the fishing suburb of
Le Pollet. (Dieppe Museum, Dieppe, France)

The summer visitors, who included many Americans, acquired the taste for local oysters, which of course had to be eaten with an ivory knife to be properly appreciated. They gaped at the picturesque costume of the inhabitants of the suburb of La Pollette, who were supposed to be the descendants of colonists from the south of France and who wore baggy breeches, wide seaman's jackets with large buttons, and picturesque bonnets. The Polletais, who were mostly fishermen, appear in many ivory carvings often as the spinning figures that balanced on one toe and that could be whirled round and round. Even fashion played into the hands of the ivory carvers; shirt buttons became a conspicuous part of men's dress, and now skilled craftsmen such as Belletete IV could earn as much as a franc for every button they made, and they could turn out 100 a day.

The strongest influence in the revival of Dieppe ivory carving, however, came from the Dieppois themselves. "There exists amongst a certain class of these people," wrote Vitet, a historian of Dieppe, in 1845, "an innate aptitude for works of sculpture, whether in ivory or in wood." He refers his readers to the woodwork of Normandy churches. The village carpenter, not just content with furnishing his church with a plain set of pews, as in other provinces, had covered them with carved flowers, garlands, and ribbons. "You will see children during their apprenticeship hollowing, opening out, and whittling ivory with a readiness and skill which are quite distinctive and which will confound you."

The innate genius of the Dieppois for art could often only be exercised if great difficulties were overcome. This was the case with Philippe Graillon, the son of a poor widow, who began life in great poverty helping his mother to make cakes of chalk, which he would then carry round on his back from door to door. While carrying out this humble task he stopped, looked into the window of an ivory carver's shop, and decided that his real vocation in life was to be a sculptor. Only after years of struggling were he and his family rescued from starvation by Blard, who

Dieppe figures, such as this hurdy gurdy man, which stood on one foot, were often given a mounting which converted them into spinning toys or *balancelles* as they were called.

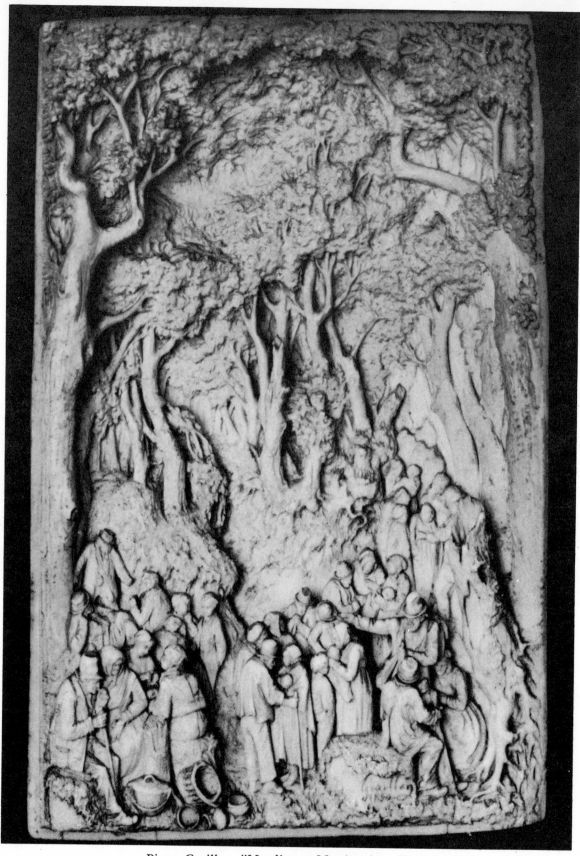

Pierre Graillon, "Mendicants Meeting in a Forest," 19th century. (Dieppe Museum, Dieppe, France)

after seeing some of Graillon's carving in alabaster, engaged him as an apprentice in his ivory workshop, giving him small ship models to be made by the dozen and patiently teaching him how to carve ivory.

For a time, the lure of studio art drew Graillon from Dieppe to Paris, where he studied in the Academies, but he decided that exhibition sculpture was not for him. Turning his back on Paris, he returned to his native town where he became one of the great masters of ivory carving of the 19th century. The essence of Graillon's work is his burning realism and his preoccupation with those who, like himself, knew the miserable side of human existence. He could be seen haunting the quays near the fishmarket, making sketch after sketch of sailors, tippling fishwives, beggars, hucksters, and tide waiters. His impressions of these unfortunates were carved straight onto the ivory, without any preliminary modeling in clay. His work is so unlike anything else done at the time that Napoleon III's award of the Legion of Honour to Graillon was probably prompted as much by the sculptor's highlighting of social problems (in which the Emperor was deeply interested) as by his portrait statuette of Napoleon.

It was unusual for anyone to be, like Graillon, a first generation ivory sculptor. Most of the other notable Dieppe sculptors belonged to ivory carving families, such as the Vitet, the Blard, the Bignard, Brunel, Colette, Guin, Norest, and Perrin. These hereditary ivory sculptors seized with both hands the opportunity offered them by the golden stream of patronage pouring into the town. Belletete IV made himself famous for his admirable profile busts in high relief (an art form that had a long history in Dieppe) till the death of his favorite apprentice broke his heart and he moved to Paris. Jacques Blard sought out the best possible models for his workmen to copy, and even placed his library at their disposal so that they might improve their style. A. Meugniot began work on a bust of the Duchesse de Berry, but Madame la Duchesse cancelled the order as soon as she had seen the preliminary

One of the favorite outlets for the Dieppe carver was the portrait in high relief. The Duchesse de Berry refused a portrait of this sort by Meugniot after she had seen the preliminary sketches. (Wallace Collection, London)

sketches. Meugniot, chagrined, later achieved his masterpiece in a portrait study where the patron could not complain: "The Old Man Dying," now in the Chateau Museum at Dieppe.

In a determination to keep up with the flood of orders that poured in, the ivory carvers took on new recruits. Buisson, who had no fewer than 24 mediocre pupils, set them all to making crucifixes. By 1824 there were nine shops selling ivory in Dieppe, by 1849 it had risen to 30, and 20 years later, although the number of shops was down to 18, there were supposed to be 96 ivory carvers at work.

It is time to take stock of the production of ivories while the art was still enjoying its heyday. Most competent critics have felt that Dieppe ivory carving never returned to the heights it had achieved during the 18th and still more the 17th centuries. Aristide Guilbert, a 19th-century observer, commented: "It is no longer the old Dieppe workmanship." Even Vitet, a local writer who might have been expected to be prejudiced in favor of his fellow citizens, may not just have been indulging in the historian's inevitable nostalgia for the past when he said that the Revolution had made an irrevocable break in the style of carving. The ease and daring of the 17th century had disappeared, and it was no longer possible to get *mosaique,* such as had been made 100 years ago. *Mosaique* was not, as its name might suggest, some kind of ivory mosaic, but what would now be called in France *travaille ajouré,* a carved fretwork of ivory worked into the very finest filigree work, in imitation of lace. Although the affinities of *mosaique* and the kind of lace that was made locally (*poussin*) must be pointed out, the basic design may have come from very far afield Russia, where this kind of decoration was the standard form of ivory carving in the Moscow and St. Petersburg workshops, or perhaps even farther away, from Siberia. Vitet goes on to say that the lacelike patterns of the fretwork have become too regular, too mechanical. There are only two aspects of the ivory carver's work that do not invite his criticism: one is the ship models, which he declares admirable; the other are purely mechanical works of skill, such as carving 13 ivory balls one within another, all of which are capable of movement.

Besides these mechanical marvels, which were, alas, much more likely to attract the customer than the finest piece of real carving or imaginative sculpture, there were the religious carvings, most of them crucifixes. These were sent out either "well finished" for those who could afford them, or "ordinary" to satisfy the rugged souls of peasants in every country. It was, no doubt, one of the "ordinary" ones that the painter Watteau had refused to kiss on his deathbed during the previous century, on the grounds that nobody had any business to portray Our Lord in such an inartistic way. While 19th-century religious carvings at Dieppe are on the whole too stereotyped to make great demands on the carver or much impression on the connoisseur, the work of the decorative carver, on the other hand, is almost invariably pleasing. This is all the more remarkable in that it covers a vast range: mirrors surrounded by flowers (one of these was ordered by the Empress Eugénie), parasol handles, hunting knife handles, fans, paper weights, paper knives, clocks, and vases.

One of the best-known products of the Dieppe carver was the Dieppe rose, beautifully exemplified in the preceding century by Saillot, who carved an exquisite spray of moss roses with every petal curling naturally and delicately from the mossy stems and serrated leaves. When the Prussians occupied Dieppe in 1871 and made themselves very unpopular by threatening to punish the town because the *maire* refused to give them unlimited free cigars from the tobacco factory, some knowledgeable enlisted man must have studied this rose in the museum, and perhaps made a sketch of it, because in 1873 a carver called Friedrich Hartmann won an award in the International Exhibition at Vienna for an ivory carving of a moss rose outlined in a spray of petals.

Of all the devices used by the Dieppe carver, none is more charming than the outline carving in miniature, set against a background of blue glass. Although this is almost certainly a British invention, and although it was first brought in by Stephany and Dresch, ivory carvers in miniature to His Majesty George III, it had a much longer life in France than in England. Indeed it lasted long enough for the historian of ivory, Alfred Maskell, to notice it and remark that the beautifully delicate carving was produced by first gluing a thin slab of ivory to a piece of wood and then sawing through the sandwich.

The only remaining kind of carving made at Dieppe that requires notice is the chess set. This could either be made in the orthodox way, with standing pieces, or be a *pique sable* set, where all the chess men were equipped with sharp spikes at the bottom so that they could be spiked into some suitable base. The name, which means "sand sticker," would suggest that originally these sets were used for playing chess on a ruled-off square on the sands of the beach. This may

Eighteenth century Dieppe work, a rose by
Saillot. French masterpieces such as this must
have inspired the Erbach masters to begin carving roses. Town Museum, Dieppe, France.

Nineteenth-century box top on a blue glass background showing a pastoral scene. (Dieppe Museum, Dieppe, France)

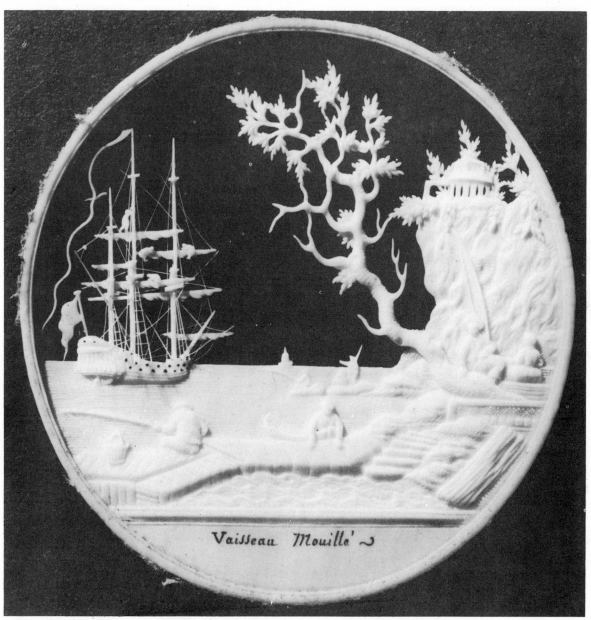

A 19th-century box top on blue glass background
from Dieppe, in the "Voyez" style. The legend
at the bottom reads: "Vaisseau Mouille." (Dieppe
Museum, Dieppe, France)

Dieppe ivory snuffbox lid. Note how the top part
of the design has been closed in.

LA CASCADE

Dieppe ivory snuffbox lid in the Stephany and
Dresch manner.

Dieppe *pique sable* chessmen. From left to right:
Knight, Pawn, Bishop, Rook.

have been the case with simple carved wooden sets used by ordinary folk, but the people who owned ivory *pique sable* sets were obviously too grand ever to sit down on a beach. Instead, like other gentlefolk in France in the 19th century, they must have sat on a chair that was placed for them on the beach by an attendant and surrounded by other attendants to keep off the common herd. Sets of this sort were often used for playing in coaches during long journeys, and they often come accompanied by a board of tatted work. This was made fairly thick, partly so as to let the chessman stick upright, but more to prevent anyone from jabbing right through the board into an opponent's knee.

The ivory carvers of Dieppe were at their best while they worked happily away, cutting, piercing, sawing, and filing, under the eyes of the public in their little shops near the entrance to the Casino, to the accompaniment of a chorus of exclamations such as: "Oh, aren't they clever" from the visitors who filled the Rue d'Agado and Grande Rue.

The rude vigor of many of their carvings, which Vitet described as "provincial rust, which intercourse with the capital has not yet rubbed off," and which had seemed so amusing to seaside visitors, attracted the sneers of the critics of the salons. When, for example, Louis Philippe ordered the famous Borghese and Medici vases, copies of classical themes on a grand scale that were to be made by Clemence and Nicolle (or according to another account by Blard), they were dismissed by the critic Chennevières as "wanting in character if not in skill," and eventually they found their way back from the Louvre, where they had been put on show, to the Museum at Dieppe, which was probably as glad to retrieve them as the Louvre was to get rid of them.

Painting by Souillot showing a 19th century
Dieppe carver at work. (Dieppe Museum,
Dieppe, France)

Not merely were the Dieppe carvers disliked as provincials who had no business in the exhibitions of the capital, the kind of ivory sculptures they were making had become unfashionable. The Dieppe carvers specialized in carvings made from nothing but ivory, but a vogue was starting for mixed ivory sculpture in combination with other materials, such as gold or bronze. Moreover Dieppe work was fairly small, but tastes in ivory were now tending toward the grandiose.

Furthermore, many critics refused to take *any* kind of ivory carving seriously, because ivory was a substance that was just as often used for furniture or cutlery or hairbrushes as for sculpture. An ivory sculptor who sent in to an exhibition was likely to find himself classed along with craftsmen who carved meerschaum pipes.

Not merely had Dieppe sculpture failed to capture the capital, it was now beginning to decline at home as well. A. Nicolle, a prominent Dieppe carver, protested against the criticisms which Chennevières had made about the Borghese and Medici vases. He asserted in 1851 that Dieppe sculpture was as good as ever, but even he was forced to admit that statuettes were

Beautiful but functional ivories, such as this parasol handle by the Frenchman J. P. Norest, 1859, depressed the status of ivory sculptors, who were often classed with craftsmen at exhibitions. (Victoria and Albert Museum, London)

difficult to sell. That, he said, was because the shopkeepers who had ordered them could not get rid of them. The decline of ivory carving was signposted by the closure of more and more ivory carving establishments. Between 1860 and 1883, the number of ivory shops fell to 15. By 1892 there were only 11, by 1900 only eight, and by 1965 there were only two carvers still at work. In every decade at least one of the old carving families died out or gave up the business, a heartrending process that, however, ensured that some of the best carvings to which the ivory sculptors had clung as family treasures went to the museum as a result of bequest or bankrupt sales.

Various factors had contributed to this decline. The rich English and Russian families, as well as the Americans, Greeks, Norwegians, Germans, Danes, and Italians, who had thronged the terrace in front of the *Etablissement des Bains,* or who had watched the bathing men helping ladies into the water ("with a tender gallantry, mingled with imperturbable gravity," says an observer of 1871 "they perform their office, carrying their light burdens down to the water's edge, dipping them with a gentleness that our Amazonian bathing women could hardly equal."), had now moved further afield to frequent other holiday centres opened up by improved communications. Political events, such as the fall of the Second Empire, had brought about a loss of custom. Ivory carving was very much a luxury industry, and events such as the revolution of 1830 could produce a ten percent drop in takings. The occupation of Dieppe by a Prussian army had driven visitors away and also disrupted the activity of the carvers. Substitutes for ivory, such as celluloid, and later on terra cotta, had begun to appear alongside ivory in the carver's windows, and because they were so much less expensive people bought them in preference to it. The advent of the steamship had robbed one of the carver's most popular products, the ivory ship model, of much of its topical appeal, though it continued to be made. Ivory carving had never required an indentured apprenticeship with the necessity of passing into a mastership at the end of the indentures. Anyone could become an ivory carver who wished to, and any foreman carver could have as many apprentices as he liked. During the boom in ivories too many people had wanted to become carvers, and too many apprentices had been engaged. Because there was no real organization among the carvers, shopkeepers had been able to force prices down, making it exceedingly difficult for the ivory sculptors to make a living. For various reasons, probably chiefly owing to the expensive nature of the material they worked in, the carvers seem to have been in a state of dependence on the shopkeepers, who dictated to them the kinds of ivories they were to produce.

The end of the Dieppe ivory industry was rather like the end of jet carving in Whitby, England, another luxury craft trade making products that would be sold to seaside tourists. Some carvers emigrated, such as Charles Tranquille Colette, who moved to London and opened a shop in Shaftesbury Avenue, marrying an English girl in the process, Dailly, and P. A. Bouteiller. Some, like Buisson, died in the poorhouse. Others dropped their standards of carving so drastically that there was no longer any money to be made out of ivory carving, unless, like Perrin of Paris, who was always trying to tempt Nicolle away from Dieppe, you set up a factory for making fake medieval statues and "aged" them with tea and tobacco juice.

Philippe de Chennevières had noted the change from small *bibelot* (table ornament) ivory sculpture to that on a grander scale. Chennevières had been invited by the sculptor Simart to a preview of his chryselephantine statue, which was to be a sort of recreation of the statue of Minerva by Phidias, a work that was as familiar to all students of classical antiquity as was Jupiter Olympias, made by the same sculptor in the same materials, ivory and gold. Quatremere de Quincy, a French archaeological savant, had spent 30 years collecting information about these statues, and in his book, *Olympian Jupiter, or the History of Gold and Ivory Sculpture,* written in 1815, he described how, in his opinion, the sculptor Phidias had been able to fit together the many pieces of ivory necessary to construct the large areas of flesh in these mammoth statues.

Simart was not attempting anything so huge as the Jupiter of the Parthenon, but his Minerva, of which he gave Chennevières a glimpse in 1855, was over life size and apparently impressive enough. Chennevières was completely entranced by "the mellow beauty, the splendid and vivid transparencies of this noble material," and by the play of light on "the head and neck, made of a single piece of ivory, set between three different shades of gold, those of the helmet, the cuirass, and the tunic." He concluded his survey of the history of ivory carving with the remark that "This poor art of ivory sculpture, which the academic sculptors have disdained for so long, has in our time (i.e. 1857) come back into singular favour." Although at some salons in the past he had been pained to note "Not one single ivory sculptor, nothing but makers of snuff boxes," in 1849 Auguste Barre had exhibited a charming statue of Rachel, and now M. de Triqueti was making ready to exhibit his.

The history of ivory carving in modern times contains many false dawns, such as the one that Chennevières was prophesying for the art in France. Had he been less sanguine, he might have commented on the fact that Simart had not even done his own ivory carving for the Minerva statue. The work had been handed out to a *practicien* or journeyman (carver) by the goldsmith, Froment Meurice, with whom he had placed the order.

As if to justify Chennevières' optimism, French ivory carving experienced a late flowering caused in part by the Belgian revival and associated with the name of Théodore Rivière, whose group "Salammbo before Matho," now in the Luxembourg, is one of the most powerful pieces of combination sculpture ever made. With Rivière, the tradition of fine ivory carving that went back to Carolingian times ended in France and the state of the art today can be summed up in the words of one of the last two remaining *ivoiriers* of Dieppe, M. Tranquille Colette, grandson of Charles Tranquille Colette. Having reached the age of 77, this veteran Dieppe carver can look back on what ivory sculpture was like in the 19th century.

"Ivory carving in France is very different from what it was in the last century. We are forced to make series of carvings which are identical, so as to be able to earn our living, besides which, competition from Hong Kong compels us to keep prices very low. What is more, patrons no longer want to collect really beautiful ivories, which, because they are of superior quality, are priced very highly.

Early 20th-century ivory carver, M. Tranquille Colette, at work.

"There are still a few ivory carvers in Paris who carry on the tradition, but we do not take on any apprentices, as our calling does not hold out any great hopes for the future."

Belgium

The connection between the Congo and Belgium, which was productive of considerable state encouragement to ivory carvers, is symbolized by a very ambitious but successful medallion commemorating the annexation of the "Free State" by Belgium, carved by Floris de Cuyper. On the obverse a personification of Belgium joins hands with the Congo before Justice, who holds a book of the laws and a sword. On the reverse the two countries look at a smaller medallion of the heads of the two men who had begun Belgium's adventure in Africa, the American explorer Henry Morton Stanley, and King Leopold of the

The personification of Belgium shows the Congo a medallion of the American explorer Henry Morton Stanley and King Leopold of the Belgians, who commissioned Stanley's explorations. (*Musée Royal de l'Afrique Centrale,* Tervuren, Belgium)

Belgians.

Many of the works of the state-patronized Belgian sculptors are of the highest technical as well as artistic interest, such as the very large busts undertaken by Thomas Vinçotte, Alfred Courtens, and Franz Huygelens. These sculptors are all well known, apart from their ivory work. Vinçotte was a veteran Belgian sculptor who worked in modified classical styles and was particularly renowned for his busts. Alfred Courtens and Franz Huygelens were amongst the most

distinguished of Vinçotte's pupils. In spite of the eminence of this trio, I feel that they overestimated their powers in attempting ivory portrait sculpture on such a grand scale. In order to get the massive blocks required for the busts (Vinçotte's head of King Leopold II stands 28 centimetres high), large pieces of ivory have been fastened together and the joins are painfully evident, indeed in Courtens's work the whole bust appears to be falling apart. Because ivory sculpture is seen at its best when every part of

A massive bust of Leopold III by Alfred Courtens, the famous Belgian sculptor. (*Musée Royal*)

A bust of King Albert I by the Belgian sculptor,
Franz Huygelen. (*Musée Royal*)

"The Embrace Of The Swan," by the Belgian
sculptor Philippe Wolfers. A characteristic piece
of combination sculpture. The vase, a lightly engraved tusk, is entwined by a bronze swan, which
rests on a colored marble pedestal. (*Musée Royal
de l'Afrique Centrale,* Tervuren, Belgium)

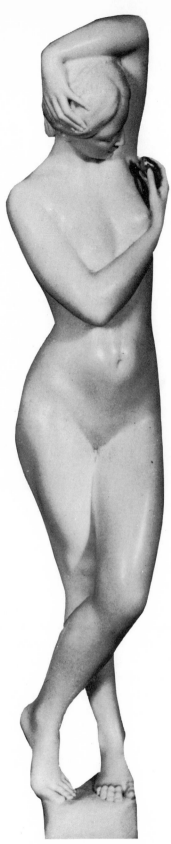

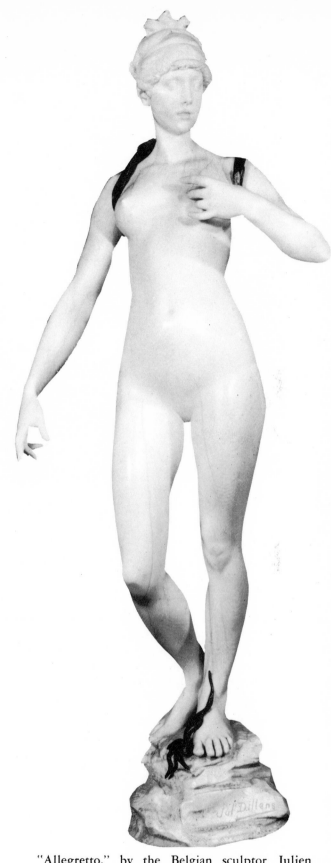

Statue by Philippe Wolfers, "The First Jewel."
(*Musée Royal de l'Afrique Centrale,* Tervuren,
Belgium)

"Allegretto," by the Belgian sculptor Julien
Dillens. A combination work in which an ivory
statue, with bronze enrichments, stands on a
marble base. (*Musée Royal*)

"Uilenspeigel," by the Belgian sculptor Charles
Samuel. Another combination statue in the decorative style in which the white ivory of the statue
contrasts with the dark marble of the pedestal.
(*Musée Royal*)

a carving reflects light on every other part,
straight join lines of this sort detract very much
from a carving's appeal by dividing it up into
compartments so that it cannot be viewed as a
whole. These busts are, in effect, just another
and an unsuccessful attempt to revive the monumental ivory carving practiced by the Greeks.
It seems impossible not to conclude either that
the methods used by classical sculptors to obtain
a join between two pieces of ivory were technically much more advanced than those at our disposal, or that the dimness of a Greek temple
prevented anyone noticing the joining lines.

Some of Phillippe Wolfer's work is also experimental in nature. His "Swan's Caress" com-
bines the formal classicism of a bronze casting
with the bizarre shape of a tusk whose only
ornament is a light scrimshawed line not blacked
in. In another example Wolfer has achieved a
masterpiece in ornamental sculpture by combining an ivory statuette set on a marble pedestal
and a baroque pearl. The title, originally "The
First Jewel," was later changed to "The Woman
With The Pearl." This work, dated 1907, is
probably the last important piece in the combination movement.

Like the preceding piece "Gladness," the
work of famous decorative sculptor Julien Dil-

lens is ornamental. It is also erotic, but with the eroticism of the Italian Renaissance, which had a strong influence on the Antwerp school to which Dillens belonged. It also reveals another preoccupation of the Antwerp sculptors, a feeling for craftsmanship.

The work of Charles Samuel, who lived well on into the 20th century, must conclude this survey of what, surely, was one of the most gifted of all European schools of ivory carving. Samuel was chiefly noted for his monuments, and he had an intimate relationship with the work shown here because he had already made a sculptural monument to the author of *Tyl Eugenspiel,* Charles de Coster.

Chapter 5.
Russia

The American reader will probably find Russian ivory carving more interesting than that of any other European school, simply because it is the one that has most in common with his own folk art. Some of the walking cane handles and fittings for embroidery turned out by Russian peasants might well have been made by the scrimshoners, and it has already been mentioned that one piece of Russian peasant art, a chessman, was actually illustrated as a piece of scrimshaw work in a very learned publication. The olive branch pattern, which is one of the mainstays of the scrimshaw decorator, first appears on a box of carved walrus ivory from Archangel.[1] Boxes such as the one I have just mentioned are of extreme interest in Russian art, because many of them[2] bear the dot and circle pattern, which is one of the most characteristic forms of Eskimo decoration. It is engraved in black line on the sides of the box, in scrimshaw fashion, and it shows that while Eskimo art influenced

American scrimshoners to the west, it affected Russia in a similar way to the east. As we shall see in a moment, the Russians are quick to disclaim any Eastern influence whatsoever on their carving. It arose, says the official Russian publication on the subject, in response to influences from Great Russia, the European part of the Russian Empire. The Russians, in fact, are probably the last people to remain convinced that it is a good thing to be European.

The strongest connection between Russian and American carving, however, does not lie in the fact that the two countries share artistic influences, that ultimately derive from the Arctic nomads inhabiting both sides of Bering Strait, so much as from the fact that they share common sources of raw material consisting of two kinds of ivory, mammoth and walrus.

Some of the ivory used in Russian carving came from a layer of fossil mammoth tusks that runs across the Bering Strait into American territory at Escholz Bay. "Here," states an account of 1873, "the cliffs are said to be either ice, or partly coated with ice, and on the top of them, embedded in, and partly coated by, the boggy or sandy soil, are numberless bones that have lost but little of their animal matter, hair being dug up with them, and the whole island having a charnel house smell."

Although some of this American mammoth ivory was to find its way to Europe, the ivory

---

1. *Connoisseur* Special Number, "Peasant Art in Russia," edited by Charles Holme, 1912, Great Russia, no. 171. Although no date is given for this box it appears by comparison with specimens illustrated in *Severorusskaya reznaya kost* ("Carved bones of Northern Russia"), I. N. Uchanova, 1969, to date from about 1730. Other similar boxes appear to have variants of the same pattern.

2. E.g. nos. 171, 172, & 176 in the *Connoisseur*, issue just cited.

Russian ivory, a box of walrus tusk made in Archangel. Note the olive branch pattern design scrimshawed on the band running round the box immediately under the lid. The early date of this box, which by comparison with similar pieces is about 1730, suggests that it was here in Russia that this particular scrimshaw design emerged.

mines on the Russian side of the Strait were a much more important source of supply for ivory sculptors. They had been laid down during the Pleistocene Age, when the mammoth, a climatic exile in Siberia when the last ice age thawed, had lain down to die in a holocaust of the species whose survival in racial memory may have given rise to the later legend of the "elephants' graveyard," where the great beasts went when they knew that they were about to perish. It was only recently that the German ivory carver, Kurt Degen, used just this phrase to describe the fossil ivory deposits.

The mammoth, a gigantic prehistoric proto-elephant covered with shaggy red hair and en-dowed with tusks 16 feet long, had been hunted all over Europe by the men of prehistory who fashioned beautiful carvings from the tusks of their slain enemy. There must have been many more ivory carvers about then than now, and it seems safe to conclude that most people in America and Europe number one somewhere among their ancestors. Perhaps this is what has implanted the liking for a good ivory carving that is present in most of us.

The passing of the mammoths had been so quick that many of them were frozen in the middle of a hearty browse on forage, and re-mained with their ivory and flesh in such perfect condition that they yielded a meal to starving

The Mammoth (*elephas primigenius*) Siberian breed.

hunters hundreds of thousands of years later, an incredible fact that somehow becomes much more credible after the first bite of Russian bread. Of course not all mammoth tusks were preserved in such perfect condition; many became badly decayed or developed the most common fault of mammoth ivory, a split into concentric or spiral rings. However, because a mammoth tusk is so large in the first place (one pair described by the German zoologist Pfizenmayer weighed 500 pounds, about five times the weight of the average African elephant tusks), even if it is badly decayed it may contain as much ivory as a sound elephant tusk. Though it had served as a quarry for ivory carvings for centuries, Siberia still contained immense quantities of tusks by the start of the 19th century. Along the whole shoreline of the province between the mouth of the Obi and Bering Strait, frozen bodies of mammoths were exposed by melting ice in warm summers or wherever sea cliffs or river banks had been washed away. The Bear Islands and the New Siberian Islands, which were favorite collecting places, were found to be positively sown

with mammoth remains when the Wrangell Expedition visited them in 1808. Between 1825 and 1831, 2,000 *poods,* or 71,000 pounds, of mammoth ivory were brought to one market alone, Yakutsk, and by 1908 this figure had become that of the annual output of fossil ivory for northeastern Siberia.

The work of collecting mammoth tusks was quickened by the arrival in Siberia of drove after drove of exiles, most of them political offenders, but others who were members of a fanatical sect of self-castrators called *Skoptsi,* whose activities bade so fair to solve the Russian problem for good that successive governments sent all those who could be caught down the long road to the east. So geared to convict life did Siberia become that when the St. Petersburg Academy of Science wrote to a district officer for information about the flora and fauna of his area, he replied, "There was a student from Warsaw called Flora Tvardezkaya here about five years ago, but the police know nothing at all about any woman called Fauna."

The pittance that these exiles were paid

(about 18 roubles a month) was quite insufficient to keep them alive, so they had to live by collecting fossil ivory and selling it for ridiculously low sums to the dealers—American, Russian, and German—who came to Siberia to buy it.

Long before the first Cossacks had ridden into Siberia in the 17th century and claimed it for the Czar, the people of the country—Eskimos, Lapps, Koryaks, Yakuts, Lamuts, and Tungus—had been making magnificent carved ivory models and engravings. Several of these models appear in the official Russian publication on carved ivory, but the titles given them are a little misleading. They do not say "These carvings were made by the Yakuts or Koryaks," though it is obvious by the style that they were. They are simply entitled "Archangel, a *genre* scene, 1820–1830," or "Camp of a northern tribe." The implication is that they were made by Russian carvers, and this implication is reinforced by the publication's statement that carving spread from Moscow and Novgorod to the north. American readers who look at the collection of Koryak and Yakut carvings in the American Museum of Natural History in New York, however, will probably be more impressed with them than the Russians appear to be, and will notice certain tricks of the nomad carver that turn up in the

Another decorative motif derived by the Russians from the Siberians—the flat, spiky tree branch. Left is from a nomad model in the State Museum of Ethnography of the Peoples of the USSR; right is from a Russian carving of the Battle of Pultawa in the State Hermitage Museum. This cultural debt has never been acknowledged.

output of Russian ivories. One is the flat spiky rendering of tree foliage, which is copied quite clearly by two carvings by Russians in the Hermitage Museum, "Abraham's Sacrifice," and "The Battle of Poltava." We will notice another important debt owed to the nomad by the Russian carver in a moment.

It is not surprising that Russian art carving should have been influenced by the Siberians, because after all it was from them that the Russians had obtained their tusks in the first place. The Siberians regarded the mammoth with superstitious dread as an "earth animal" that burrowed beneath the ground and made the tundra shake. They regarded the finding of a new mammoth carcass as a piece of bad luck, and they sometimes fell ill with nervous prostration after they had made the discovery. Economic considerations have a habit of overcoming superstitious feelings, however, as when one goes off to work on the 13th of every month, and the Siberians soon found that mammoth tusks had a ready sale southwards in China as well as eastwards in Russia.

"We may read about the digging vole of the north," wrote that great connoisseur of the arts, the Chinese emperor Kang Hsi, who lived between 1661 and 1721. "Its other names are: 'the hidden mouse,' and 'mother of mice.' Far in the north, in the land of the Russians, these rats, as large as elephants, live in the ground. When air or sunlight touch them, they die immediately. There are digging voles which weigh up to ten thousand pounds. Their teeth are like those of elephants, and the people of the north make vessels, combs, knife handles, and other articles out of them. I have seen such teeth myself, and the things made from them." So Siberian carving was well known to the Chinese at least as early as the 17th century.

The objects made by the nomads took the form of reindeer, dogs, sledges, *yurts* (wigwam-like tents of skins), trees, and the nomads themselves. Some of them were made in fresh or fossil ivory, the rest in mammoth. Like the carvings of the New Stone Age folk, and like those

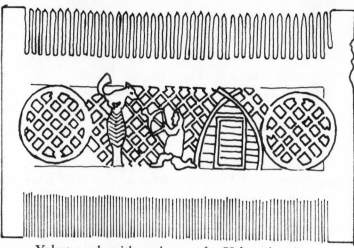

Yakut comb with a picture of a Yakut shooting a sable. Note the background pattern of *mosaique*. This kind of *mosaique* appears again and again in Russian carving, though the Russians also evolved their own asymmetrical mosaique. Probably the Yakuts preferred this kind because four is their sacred number, so a four-sided pattern would be holy.

of the whalers, the nomad carvings were intended to bring good luck in hunting. Reference to this superstitious habit amongst whalers may surprise some readers, but aboard British whalers on the Northern Fishery, a garland containing a model ship was solemnly raised to the masthead on the first of May, that is, when the whaler had got into her hunting ground. In the same way, the nomads believed their ivory carvings would bring them good luck, with a little help from their medicine man or shaman. While on a visit to a Lamut village, Pfizenmayer watched the shaman going through his rituals. On the walls of the tent were hung the figures of men and animals carved from wood, mammoth ivory, fossil, rhinoceros horn, and the roots of plants. These symbolized the spirits whose assistance the shaman needed to secure good fortune and good health for the tribe. During the ceremony he sprinkled them repeatedly with reindeer blood and perfumed the carvings with the smoke of cedar-gum mixed with powdered herbs, so that eventually the whole tent was filled with stupefying fragrance.

Besides models, the nomads made rings, combs, powder horns, matchboxes, knife handles, and boxes ornamented in fine fretwork. A very delicate fret tracery, in which figures and ornaments are suspended and surrounded by a network of ivory, is characteristic of Yakut work. This very distinctive style of decoration seems to have passed directly into European Russian carving and eventually to other parts of Europe. A comb in the Russian State Museum[3] is virtually identical with a Yakut comb[4] save for the fact that the silhouette figures surrounded by the fretwork are those of a fine lady and gentleman in the Russian example, while in the Yakut one, they are a Yakut and a sable that he is hunting.

Fretted work appears in Great Russian peasant carvings of the 17th and 18th centuries. In what

3. No. 17 in *Severorusskaya.* "Comb." Second half of the 18th century. Russian State Museum. Although the piercings in the Russian comb are rounded, the Yakut square piercings are imitated in other Russian carvings in the same periodic work, e.g. nos. 76 and 80.

4. In E. W. Pfizenmayer, *Siberian Man and Mammoth,* London, 1939, p. 184.

Another Archangel box, of the same period. Note dot and circle design taken from Eskimo art, the carved panels which recall Byzantium, and the fretwork pattern of *mosaique* along the top of the box. Russian art was the heir of the Caesars as well as the Barbarians.

might be called the "Palace Style" of the carvers who labored in the Moscow Armory Chamber workshops in the Kremlin, and in the *ateliers* of St. Petersburg, to supply the demand of the Russian aristocracy for ivory carvings it does not merely appear, it predominates. So much is fretted work the characteristic style of the whole period that out of the 82 carvings chosen to illustrate the official Russian publication on ivory —examples that cover the 17th, 18th, and 19th centuries, and which are representative of palace art as a whole, 50 contain fretwork. So it is no exaggeration to say that the Yakuts presented the Russians with their characteristic style of carving. Not all this fretwork is quite the same of course; the older, 17th-century work is very like the tracery in Islamic art. The Russians acquired some of their mammoth ivory from the Arabs,

who traded it to them in the market town of Bolgari, on the Volga, while the Tartar hordes still interrupted direct communication with the north, so it would be quite in order for Russian ivory carving to show some eastern influence. As the Russians would be under Yakut influence, because they would buy carvings as well as tusks from the Yakuts, the two traditions of fretwork seem to have reinforced one another, so that by the time we get to the 19th century the fret is characteristic of Russian carving as a whole, and it looks very like a Yakut fret with many tiny piercings that suspend swags and garlands.

Now if there is one form of ivory carving that is inevitably recalled by the description I have just given it is Dieppe *mosaique,* the local name for a pierced fretwork pattern. The two styles are so similar that there can be no doubt one derived from the other. Which came first? The only Dieppe *mosaique* still in existence dates from the 18th and 19th centuries, whereas there are plenty of 17th-century Russian examples. The resemblance between Russian fret and *mosaique* was noted by at least one French observer of the 19th century who simply attributed it to the fact that Russian noblemen must have purchased Dieppe work that afterwards found its way into the Imperial collection.

All the evidence points in the opposite direction. The *mosaique* style was brought to European Russia from Siberia. It was adopted by the Dieppe carvers after it was in vogue in Russia, probably after some visiting Russian *boyar* had left a snuffbox to be repaired in the little Norman town, or specified that another, just like the one he had left as a copy, must be made as a present for a friend.

The thesis that I have just put forward is a completely novel one, and it may surprise some readers to learn that a design traveled 6500 miles and became the characteristic style of four countries (as we shall see when we come to Germany, *mosaique* was introduced there too by Kehrer). Russian ivory carving is such an unexplored field, however,[5] that almost any discovery made about it is bound to be novel. Good ideas have wings, and it is much easier to adopt one that comes from thousands of miles away than from the blank wall of your studio just a few feet away as you wonder whatever to carve next.

The Dieppe carvers, moreover, had a genius for adaptation. They had taken over the idea of ultra-miniature sculpture from Stephany and Dresch.[6] They had taken over another of their

principal kinds of carving, the ivory ship, from the Norwegians.[7] They had copied the concentric ivory pierced spheres with other movable globes within, a device that was originally Chinese but that was, incidentally, copied in Russia as well.

Carving in European Russia had been started by the same folk who had bequeathed their talents to the Normandy carvers—the Vikings. The first ivory trader to appear in history is a Viking called Othere, who called to pay his respects to Alfred the Great of Wessex and presented him with some walrus teeth that he had just brought back from Perm in northern Russia. By the tenth century a flourishing ivory carving industry had begun among the settlers from Novgorod who had colonized Pomorye. They were joined in the 15th century by many incomers from Moscow. Archangel and Kholmogory became the great centres of carving, and many ivory sculptors moved from these outlying provinces to the two capitals of Russia, St. Petersburg and Moscow, which were spots ideally suited for plying a luxury trade such as marketing ivories.

As has already been mentioned, Russian carving seems to have been divided between walrus ivory (either the fossil "beach" variety from tusks washed up on the shores of Bering Strait, whose tones range from creamy brown to purplish black, or fresh ivory from walrus hunted in Siberia or Alaska)[8] and mammoth ivory. The latter variety certainly predominated in the very large pieces that are prominent among the works of "palace art" at which we are now going to look.

---

5. It is striking that the article on "Ivory Carving," in the *Encyclopaedia Britannica* makes no reference to Russian work at all while Alfred Maskell, in his classic work "Ivories," devotes just five pages, out of a total of more than 500, to the subject.

6. Eugen von Philippowich's splendid work, "Elfenbein," gives two other examples of workers in Mikroschnitzerei, Francesco Tanadei (1770–1828) in Turin, and J.J. von Bilang, a Swede who had served in the French army (1740–1805). Both of them seem much less likely sources for this style than the London carvers just across the Channel.

7. So far as I know the first ivory ship made is the "Norwegian Lion," carved by the Norwegian sculptor Jakob Jensen Nordmand in 1654 and now in Schloss Rosenborg, Copenhagen.

8. Although the official Russian work on ivory *Severorusskaya reznaya kost,* which has been referred to more than once, says firmly that it is a history of *bone* carving, there can be no doubt that the majority of the pieces it illustrates are made of mammoth or walrus ivory, whatever the translator says. Some of the works illustrated are too big to be made from any kind of bone; others, for examples, have been already described in the *Connoisseur* special issue (nos. 177 & 176) and are referred to there as being "in carved walrus ivory from Archangel."

This style exists on two levels—the successful and the mediocre. The latter is usually the result of a dogged attempt by some peasant carver to work in the classical representational style borrowed from the west. "Russians are told," remarked the Prince de Ligne, "to become sailors, huntsmen, musicians, engineers, or artists, and they become them, for such is their master's will." This well-meant desire to please the master resulted in some really shocking work during the 19th century, such as A. Korzhavin's "Model of the monument to Minin and Pozharsky,"[9] or the even more atrocious "Model of the monument to M. V. Lomonosov."[10] When the carvers attempted a direct copy from the work of a foreign ivory sculptor, such as a snuffbox with a portrait of General Kutusov and a battle scene, which is obviously modeled on a Dieppe blue glass box, the result is even more unfortunate.

Left to himself, however, the Russian carver escaped from the trammels of western-style representational art, which had imposed a dummy-like rigidity on his figures, and began to work in his own style. He seemed endowed both with limitless inspiration and the technical ability to carry out whatever his whimsical imagination suggested to him.

No type of work is more indicative of the Russian genius than the chess set, which so often in the West degenerates into a stereotyped set of abstract forms or worse still a set of turned pieces, competent but cold. In Russia every chessman is an ivory carving in its own right, and as the forms of the Russian set were much more decorative than those of the West to begin with (take for example the rook, which is usually a ship with all sails set), the carver had considerable scope for his talent.

But it is in the deployment of *mosaique* that the ivory sculptor shows what he is made of. Often, as a concession to the westernizing taste of the aristocracy, the work will be a composite

9. No. 82 in "Severorusskaya."
10. Ibid., no. 71.

Russian chessmen: a King and a Rook.

one. There will be an ikon or a portrait *bas relief* or a medallion of Alexander I in the centre of the piece, and all the rest will be filled up with purely decorative carving.

It is advisable to know something about the practical side of ivory carving before one can appreciate the works of Nikolay Stephanovich Vereschagin (1770–c. 1814), the greatest Russian *mosaique* carver of the 19th century.

If you show an ivory carver any kind of open work carving—such as the cut outs that I make myself—his first question will probably be "Did you use a support?" That is, did you glue down the very thin ivory on a wooden backing before you carved it? If a carver does not use a support, he is much more likely to break the ivory tracework and he will consequently need to develop much more technical skill. Vereschagin used rounded and cone-shaped sections in his work that must not only have been virtually impossible to support, but which must, from the position in which they had to be held, have been very difficult to carve.

The master's work was mostly commissions from the Czar to make gifts to be carried to foreign princes, and especially Eastern potentates, by Russian ambassadors. It is not surprising,

Vases by Nikolay Stephanovich Vereschagin,
1770–c.1814.

then, that his ivories tend to be in the grand manner. The St. Petersburg sculptor's masterpiece is probably the State Museum Vase. It is constructed on the lines of an incense burner and rests on a massive plinth; the bottom part, solid to the hemisphere, is carved with classical decorative motifs. The cover of the vase is surmounted by a knob that is copied from Catherine II's equestrian monument to Peter the Great. The tiny figure of Peter perched on his enormous rock makes a very unsuitable finial for such a large carving. Large medallions of rural scenes ornament the sides of the vase. These are carved solid, a departure from Vereshchagin's earlier practice, shown in the vases in the State Historical Museum and State Hermitage, where the medallions on the sides were *ajouré* or opened out in *mosaique* style. I feel myself that the solid medallions have a much less happy effect than their pierced predecessors, but obviously Vereshchagin is experimenting with the contrast between the solid parts of the vase and the *mosaique,* which, like the fretted dome of some Eastern temple, runs up the hemisphere of the vase surmounting a legend of words in delicate tracery.

There are no masters of the stamp of Vereshchagin during the remainder of the 19th century. Palace art began to decline around the 1850s, though ivory carvings continued to be made for the luxury market down to 1917. While it lasted, it had been a very diversified school of carving, producing combs, coffers, goblets, furniture, needle cases, and many other kinds of carvings. It is in works such as the Vereshchagin

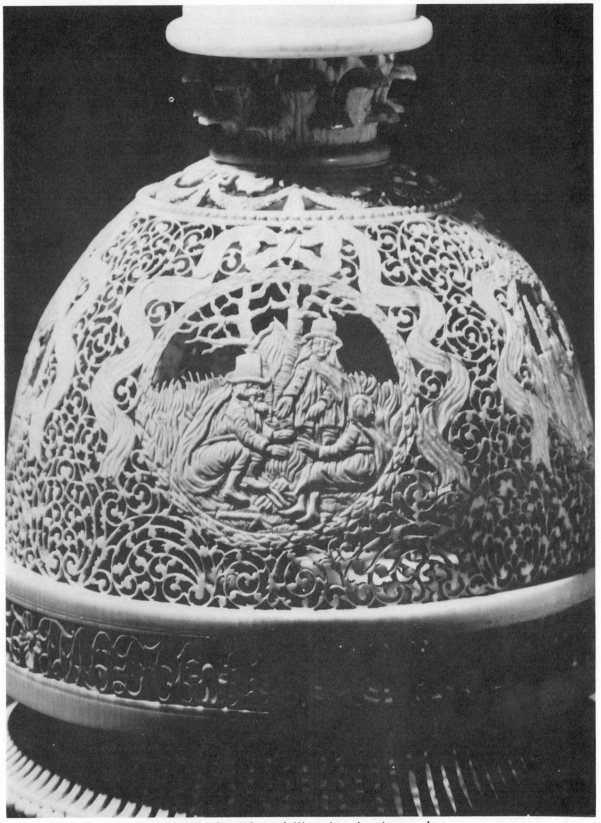

Detail of solid medallion in *ajouré* vase by
Vereschagin. Peasants warming themselves in the
fields.

Vase in "Palace Style," late 18th to 19th century.

Dressing table mirror, 18th to 19th century.
(Russian State Art Collections, Moscow)

Dressing table mirror, 18th century. (Russian
State Art Collections, Moscow)

vases, the miniature chests of drawers, dressing table mirrors, and secretaires, in which *mosaique* predominates, that the art of Old Russia lives on at its best. If it is enough for an ivory carver to be purely decorative, then it is impossible not to award Russian carving during the 19th century a very high place among the European schools, perhaps the highest.

Although palace art declined, the Siberian nomads continued to work in their traditional style down to the outbreak of the first world war. Czarist Russia, and later on the Soviets, tried to re-educate both Siberian and peasant carvers in the principles of Western-style representational art. The Soviet government trading agency, Amtorg, marketed their work abroad.

The present-day Soviet carver, working in places like Kholmogory and Lomonosov, tends to specialize in the production of statuettes of children and animals, often of a rather sentimental sort, but probably quite as near to popular taste in the West as in Russia and certainly no worse made than shop ivories anywhere else, although apparently made, as in the West, with the help of power tools. It is of course a great credit to Russia to have maintained an ivory carving industry at all, at a time when ivory carving is on the decline in other countries. Backed by apparently inexhaustible supplies of mammoth ivory, and fired by a thousand-year-old tradition, there seems no reason why Russian carvers should not try to recover some of the heights they reached in the past.

Chapter 6.
Germany

To the ancient Germans, the forest was a holy place, the source of inspiration and teaching. It has maintained this role in the life of the modern German ivory carver, who tends to live in a district called Odenwald, or "Odin's Wood," at a tiny hamlet called Erbach, set in smiling woodlands. With such surroundings, modern carving in Germany has always been much more of a peasant art than, say, the very sophisticated carvings made there from the Middle Ages to the 18th century, which smack of the palace, cathedral town, or walled city in which most of them were produced. Modern German carving has been practical and marketable, and its makers have always been much more concerned with what their patrons will buy than with what the critics will say. Simple folk themselves, they have never hesitated to exploit simple, even naive motifs drawn from their native forest, such as the Erbach stags, which pace delicately through so many carvings, or the even more famous Erbach roses. If a critic were to ask one of these carvers "Don't you ever get tired of carving roses? Why don't you do something new?" no doubt he would have replied: "Does Nature ever get tired of producing roses? She doesn't seem to have the urge to be doing something new all the time, neither do I."

Peasants are hardheaded as well as unsophisti-cated, however, and the Erbachers have never hesitated to move with the times. They reluctantly adopted machinery to make their carvings, and were thus able to continue production while Geislingen in Wurtemburg, which used to be a much more famous center than Erbach, had to give up ivory carving altogether. Moreover, they realized the value of advertisement and competed in international exhibitions, winning many prizes. The fact that the prize-winning works had been made by peasants was in itself an inducement to many people to buy them. Lots of people felt it was much more creditable for a humble countryman to have produced a fine carving than for an artist trained in the academies. The Erbachers also traveled in other countries looking for new ideas for carvings. Some of them must have exchanged their sculptor's blouses for the regulation Prussian field gray when they were called up for the war of 1870 with France. As I have already said, they brought back with them, from occupied Dieppe, the famous Erbach rose. In 1873 an ivory rose sculpted by the Erbach carver Friedrich Hartmann took a bronze medal at the International Exhibition in Vienna. The rose, successfully transplanted to Erbach, became one of the most popular types of carving there, and a much more lasting trophy of the war of 1870 than even the German Empire

"Pair of Stags," by Otto Glenz, 1930–1948.
Alongside the Rose, the Stag has been the most
popular, and the longest lasting, motif at Erbach.
(Private collection)

itself.[1]

Although they were in touch with other
countries, the Erbachers kept their feet firmly
planted on their workroom floors and refused to
be swept away by current fashions that were unsuitable for Erbach. One of these was the combination sculpture movement that dominated
Europe in the 1890s and produced a crop of
mixed bronze and ivory carvings in most countries, even Germany, where Max Klinger did a
statue of Beethoven in marble, bronze, and ivory.
The Erbachers saw no difficulty in combining
their ivories with gold and silver; they had always had a strong connection with the neigh-

boring town of Hanau, which has been a center
for German jewelers for a long time, and Otto
Glenz constructed ivory and silver platters, in
which, however, the silver is kept to a minimum.
The ivory carvers were not going to turn themselves into bronze casters, and Glenz's statue
"Elfe," made between 1895 and 1910, breathes
the very spirit of the Combination movement,
but is a work of pure ivory, without any bronze
fittings.

So many of the peasant virtues cluster about
the Erbach school—fondness for nature, patient
and unhesitating craftsmanship inspired by a
natural taste for design working through traditional forms, economical use of material, and a
determination to overcome all difficulties (exemplified by the sculptors working in Erbach
today, several of whom have spent years in Russian prison camps)—that it is strange to reflect

1. A glance through Eugen von Philippowich's "Elfenbein"
will reveal a total absence of any German rose motifs before
this date. The rose must have come from somewhere, and
what center is more likely to have provided it than Dieppe,
where it was already popular?

Goblet, by F. Böhler. Successes at international exhibitions such as this exhibit, which took a high award, helped the Erbach carvers to achieve European renown. (From the *Illustrated London News*)

bach in 1781 he did not disdain to do so either. Under the direction of Johann Tobias Arzt, the master carver of the nearby town of Michelstadt, Count Francis became an ivory carver. When trouble arose between the towns of Michelstadt and Erbach, he decided he would form his own guild of ivory workers in his own principality. Seven master carvers, including his own old teacher Arzt, were formally incorporated into the guild on July 17, 1788, along with two

that it owed its beginning, not to a peasant, but a prince.

Count Francis I of Erbach-Erbach, born in 1754, was a *philosophe* who had traveled in France and agreed with Rousseau that every man should learn some kind of useful calling. Other German princes had turned ivory on the lathe, and when Count Francis returned to Er-

Erbach and Balmoral. Prince Albert, husband of Queen Victoria, dressed as a Scottish highlander, surmounts a goblet bearing scenes of hunting life. (From the *Illustrated London News*)

Goblet by Friedrich Hartmann, 1890. Drinking vessels in ivory have always been more popular in Germany than in any other country. (In the Museum Collection at Erbach)

became the first President of the Corporation, which, he was determined, should enhance the revenues of his principality as well as help him to carry on his hobby. He encouraged the ivory workers to make utilitarian objects as well as artistic carving, and set the example himself by producing as his "masterpiece," to show he had served his apprenticeship to some profit, two billiard balls and a chess set, which can still be seen in the Count's palace at Erbach. As well as work in ivory, he encouraged turnery, the use of the less expensive stagshorn, ornamented with black line engraving filled in with black wax—scrimshaw in a word—and work in mixed materials. He himself made a fine table in ivory and tortoiseshell, candlesticks in hartshorn and ivory, and some well-turned ivory boxes. Although some of the early work of the school that has been preserved, such as snuffboxes inlaid with ivory and tortoiseshell, shows a strong Italian influence, the Count himself seems to have been aware of the artistic trends that were quickening the 19th century. One of his works, an ornamental vase, is very much influenced by the Gothic revival associated with the Romantic Movement, while another, a candelstick in hartshorn and ivory, portrays the first of the Erbach stags. Under his influence the familiar Erbach motifs began to appear. Count Francis himself favored hunting scenes, while the animal painter whom he introduced to Erbach, Christian Kehrer, introduced realistic pictures of deer. Later Eduard Kehrer, the son, began a "Sunday drawing school" for the carvers, the forerunner of the Craft College for Ivory and Wood Carving founded at Erbach in 1892, which is still in existence and the only one of its kind in Europe.

It is to Eduard Kehrer, too, that we apparently owe the pierced-work jewelery that is so characteristic of Erbach in the "Biedermayer" era, which corresponds to the period when crinolines were fashionable. Most of this pierced work is naturalistic—stags, trees, and so forth—but it does contain, in addition, swags and garlands very reminiscent of those used in Dieppe *mosaique,* and I feel it is safe to conclude that here is

journeymen and two apprentices. The name of one of the apprentices, Count von Fürstenau, shows what a strong hold ivory carving had taken on the German aristocracy. Count Francis

Dish in ivory and silver, by Otto Glenz. (In the
Friederich Kolletzky Collection at Erbach)

just another manifestation of this much-traveled
style.

When Count Francis died in 1823 the school
was well established, although still overtopped
by the rival carving center at Geislingen. The
sun of Erbach started to rise during the 1840s,
however, when the ivory carvers began to turn
from the fairly functional pieces they had been
making—table settings and candlesticks—to
jewelry ornamented with groups of deer, stags,
horses, huntsmen, and hounds. No subjects could
have been more acceptable to the general taste

of the time, some of which at least radiated
from Queen Victoria's hunting castle of Balmoral, in the Scottish Highlands, where the most
important piece of sculpture was a bas relief of
the patron saint of huntsmen, St. Hubert. Just
as everything to do with hunting was fashionable
in England, so too was everything German, for
Queen Victoria's beloved husband was a prince
from a tiny German principality, Coburg. The
connection between Erbach and Balmoral is symbolized by two goblets made by Bohler. On one
of them, Prince Albert, in full Highland regalia,

helping to complete the decline of Erbach's greatest rival abroad, her great rival at home, Geislingen, declined and the workers from the Wurtemburg center flocked to Erbach, where production expanded and diversified.

Friedrich Hartmann, for example, carved statues, altar pieces, and ornamental clocks. Philip Willmann's specialties were copies from

Jug in ivory and silver, by Otto Glenz. Compare this with the Triqueti Vase to see the very different levels of achievement in combination sculpture. (Friederich Kolletzky Collection, Erbach)

presides over hunting scenes copied from the paintings of Sir Edwin Landseer.

Several generations of talented carvers, men like Ernst Kehrer, Freudenberger and Mayenscheim, Johann Michel, Friedrich Hartmann, and Philip Willman, lifted Erbach to fame. Her sculptures began to take prizes at foreign exhibitions, her carvers to travel abroad and her jewelry to be eagerly sought after in Paris and Vienna.

While German troops occupied Dieppe, thus

Goblet, about 1800 (in the same collection).

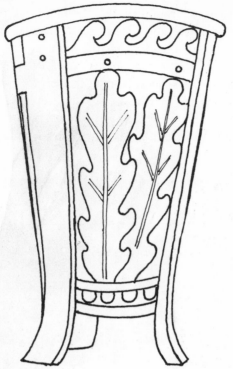

Ivory furniture made by Count Francis I of Erbach-Erbach, about 1800.

style, and kept changing to something new. His long life, from 1865 to 1948, gave him a depth of experience granted to few. He began by copying classical and baroque work and making small original carvings, such as his "Venus and Cupid," made in 1892 and exhibited at Dresden. Then

"The Three Graces," by the German carver Trumpfheller. Early Erbach work, about 1800. (Collection of Friederich Kolletzky, Erbach)

antique statues—something much nicer than it sounds, because even the most severely classical statue becomes much more attractive when reduced to a few inches high and worked in a creamy material like ivory—pendants with angel's heads between blossoms, and "hand brooches," in which a lady's hand held a lily-of-the-valley or a rose.

During the 1890s Erbach passed through a crisis. Changes in fashion demanded that carving must be simplified, and the commercial climate of ivory carving required that a change be made to mass production. Machines were installed to make series of carvings of similar design, though each piece still remained an individual work of art. Thus the school kept tradition alive, encouraged its workers to express themselves artistically, and yet was able to continue as a commercial proposition.

The culmination of Erbach carving came in the person of Otto Glenz. Like most great masters, Glenz was not satisfied with his original

"Wild Boar on a box lid," by Christian Eduard
Kehrer, 1835. Kehrer gave lessons in drawing
and helped to popularize forest scenes in Erbach.
(In the Count's Collection at Erbach)

in revolt against his youthful style he adopted a much plainer and simpler one, and became content to carve shapes without added decorative work. It is to this period that we owe "Die Muschel," one of his most tender and thoughtful works, and certainly one of the finest ivories ever made.

During the 1920s his connection with the Benedictine monastery of Beuron influenced his work yet again. When the world monetary crisis brought the demand for large pieces almost to a standstill, Glenz reverted to the traditional Erbach motifs of stags and woodland scenes.

Glenz did not stand alone in Erbach but was

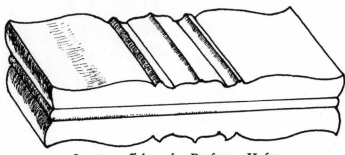

Ivory snuff box, by Professor Hofer.

"The Shell," by Otto Glenz. (In the Museum Collection at Erbach)

del; Otmar Edelbauer; Valentin Denker, well known for his chessmen; Hans Helmuth Kletetschka, a sculptor who loves to portray bagpipers and peasants working in the vineyards; and, best known of them all, Georg Frolich.

Frolich's work, like so many other distinguished carvers, was largely experimental. While in his statues he remained representational (although influenced by expressionism), that is,

"Sprite," by Otto Glenz, 1895–1910. (In the Museum Collection at Erbach)

surrounded during his last years by a bevy of talented carvers, working in styles that varied from neoclassicism to charmingly realistic animal portraiture. They included Christian Wegel, who made delightful copies from the antique, such as his "Venus de Medici," as well as jewelry and animal figures; Max Frenzel, another great *animalier;* Ludwig Walther, famous for the statue of St. George presented to Queen Elizabeth II, but probably at his best making exquisite nude figures; Josef Wendel, who carved statues, animals, and jewelry, whose talent has been inherited by his son Leonhard; Georg Wen-

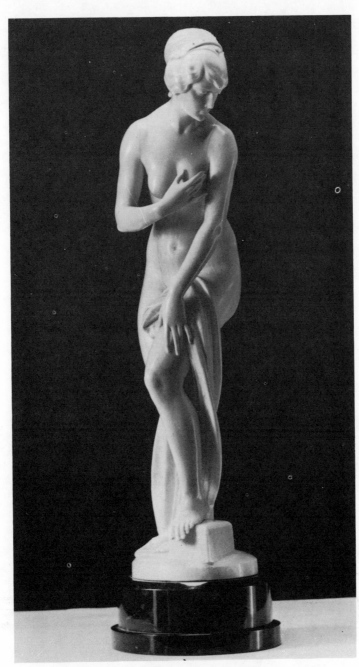

"The Bather," by Otto Glenz, 1912. (In the Museum Collection, Erbach)

"Horses," by Ludwig Walther. One of the most
forceful aspects of the genius of the Erbach
carvers is the way they can take a trite, banal
theme, like that of a procession of animals along
a tusk (familiar to everyone through its employment by African sculptors), and adapt it so that
it becomes once more full of life and vitality.
(Private Collection)

"Herd of Deer," by Ludwig Walther. The background has been carved away so as to render it
diaphanous. (Private Collection)

"St. George," by Ludwig Walther. (Presented to
Her Majesty Queen Elizabeth II by the State of
Hesse)

Steer, by Georg Frölich

utilitarian work. He makes beautiful boxes from the whole thickness of the tusk, and by some secret known only to himself, manages to avoid showing the unsightly "heart line" that runs through every central part of an elephant's tusk, even a billard ball. Adam Amend's magnificent jewelry, which is made in Hanau, reminds us of the connection between this city of goldsmiths and Erbach, which has always been strong.

The difficulty of getting recruits for the ranks

trying to transcend the mere form he was carving and give it a meaning beyond that of simple realistic portrayal, a meaning summed up by Hans Werner Hegemann as "tender monumentalism," in his jewelry he is abstract, or figurative, suggesting though not always portraying real beings or objects. Frolich's designs for his jewelry are so well thought out and so involved that they could easily be transferred from the few square centimeters of a brooch to the whole front of a vast building. Their pierced work represents the final version of Dieppe *mosaique,* which, needless to say, has not been made in Dieppe for a very long time.

Karl Schmidt Rottluf, who exchanged the palette of the painter for the graver of the ivory carver, has not lost the painter's eye, and still composes with graphic skill. Wilhelm Wegel's work began in a tender realism, as shown in his "Mother Love," but was influenced by Frolich and the contemporary German sculptor Ernst Barlach, so that during the 50s and 60s of this century it passed into a stark graphicism in which his figures, instead of being carved in the round, are outlined by deep gouge cuts.

Albrecht Glenz, son of Otto Glenz, works in stone, bronze, and wood, as well as ivory. His relief, "Freundinnen," is easily my favorite modern German work, but his work in mixed materials probably brings a greater material reward. Georg Schwinn's work illustrates another of the standbys of the ivory carver—

Mother and Child, by E. Kuhn, 1951.

of the Erbach carvers, which is felt in Germany as in other countries, has been overcome in part by the arrival of refugees from East Germany, such as Ulrich Seidenberg. Yet it is surprising that one source of recruitment for ivory carvers, made wide use of in England, has been overlooked—women. There is only one German woman carver, Hildegard Domizlaff. She makes liturgical ivories, such as bishop's croziers, crucifixes, and goblets, and her work is a fusion between expressionism and the traditional forms of religious portrayal. Her disregard for detail makes her ivories seem like precursors of those of Erich Kuhn, whose figures seem, says Hans Werner Hegemann, "like unopened human buds, surrounded by a transparent shell of ivory."

The principal changes in Erbach carving since the 1930s have been a move away from representationalism to expressionism and a dabbling in abstract forms such as Frolich's jewelry. Kurt Degen, another modern carver, feels that it is unlikely that ivory carving will ever become completely abstract, as "an organic substance, such as ivory, seems by definition incompatible with unrepresentational form." Wood, however, is an organic substance too, and it is often used for abstracts, while ivory abstracts have been made in England. Theodor Mayer, although still perhaps more figurative than abstract, has produced works of such stark simplicity that it would be difficult to realize what the subjects were without the help of the titles. So Michel Belloncle's exhortation to ivory carvers to turn to the abstract may well be answered in Germany, not France.

The German school has shown itself more daringly experimental than any other in Europe by discarding the core of the tusk for its bark, which has hitherto been stripped off and discarded. Instead of carving forms out of the core of the tusk, or sawing it into slabs for bas reliefs, some modern German carvers have sought for accidental blemishes on the outside and worked them into a design. They have, in Kurt Degen's words "abstained from any arbitrary intervention and let the natural form speak for itself." What would have been regarded as defects in a tusk by representational sculptors of the past—deep discoloration, jagged fissures, deep black cracks—and generally what ivory merchants call "staleness" in ivory have now become, in the hands of a modern master like Jan Holschuh, the present Director of Design at the Erbach *Fachschule,* its beauties. There is not enough bad elephant ivory to go round however—the outside of the average tusk presents a much more unified appearance than does the bark of a tree. Consequently, in order to get the kind of tusks that will enable them to "seize the feeling of the material and the sense of the structure, both fundamental for modern sculpture," the Erbach Expressionists have had to seek for tusks in the great mammoth mines of the north. There they have found ivory just to their liking, creviced, pitted by erosion, and deeply colored by absorption of the juices of the earth for millenia.

By contrast with the startling novelty of much of the work of Holschuh and Kuhn, which shows that new ideas can still be worked into man's oldest art form, much of the day-to-day work at Erbach seems tame. The carvers use machinery to help them make carvings—such as jewelry, chessmen, paper knives, and statuettes—in identical series. Even in commercial work of this sort pieces like Jan Holschuh's magnificent tea caddies, cups, and jars stand out, and it is easy to see that the artist has not been lost in the artisan.

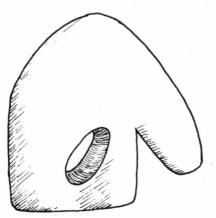

Bear, by Albert G. Theodor Mayer.

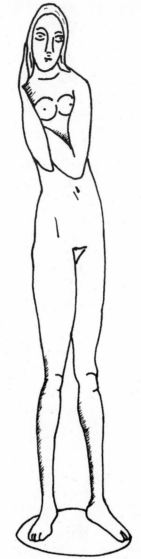

Woman, by Von. O. Ammersbach.

The commercial side of Erbach has enabled artistic ivory carving to continue and has ensured that methods of handworking, which go back to the Carolingian era, will be transmitted to each new worker, along with the techniques of the machine tool and an all-important training in aesthetics.

With a sound commercial substratum to artistic carving, a Craft College inspired by the teaching of the foremost ivory carvers of the day, an ivory museum where the contemporary worker can daily compare his achievements with those of the past, and a sympathetic acceptance of ivory carving as a living part of contemporary art,[2] German carvers can look forward to the future with more confidence than those of any other country.

2. Exemplified by Dr. Hans Werner Hegemann's very distinguished account of modern German ivory sculpture *Elfenbein in Plastik, Schmuck und Gerät.* Peters, Hanau am Main, Germany. Dr. Hegemann is Curator of the Ivory Museum at Erbach. I have based this chapter in great part on his work and on the catalogue for the exhibition at the Musée d'Art et d'histoire, Geneva, *Travaux d'Artistes et Artisans Allemands,* 1960–61, which was contributed to by Dr. Hegemann and Kurt Degen.

Chapter 7.

English Ivory Carving

There are no well-marked schools of ivory carving in England as there are in France, at Dieppe for example. Every French sculptor can be related, more or less, to every other. French ivory carving is like a tree; every twig can be traced back to the parent trunk. Most English ivory sculptors never studied their art under a master. They taught themselves to carve, and this is one of the reasons why their styles are so individual and so interesting. Because they never came under the influence of a master, they have put much more of themselves into their art than they would otherwise have done. Instruction of any kind in ivory carving in this country has only been intermittent, and has now ceased completely. Even if a particular sculptor did study with an ivory carver he would usually be quick to disclaim that he owed anything to the elder man's style. Every ivory carver is a new departure. There are no minor ivory carvings in England, nor have there been any in modern times, so there is only studio sculpture to discuss in this chapter.

One of the reasons why English ivory carvers have never labored to supply their own market with small, decorative, and functional carvings, and why even the ivory panels in the English furniture displayed at Vienna in the Exhibition of 1873 were designed by the Frenchman Lormier is that the English have always been fond of imported ivories. George Little, an American who was imprisoned for a time at Stapleton along with many Frenchmen, before being moved to Dartmoor, commented: "These French prisoners had become so thoroughly reconciled to their situation (some of them having been here six and eight years) that their minds appeared to be wholly occupied with gain. I knew many of them who, when peace was effected between France and England, had saved from one to two thousand guineas[1] and there were some who did not actually wish to leave the prison."

It was not, however, the French who benefited from this love of imported ivories so much as the Indians and the Chinese. As India was then part of the British Empire, she was given exhibition space at the Great Exhibition of 1851, and also exhibited at European International exhibitions. So far as even the British press was concerned, any effect that British exhibitors in ivory may have made was always eclipsed by the Indian Pavilion. One British journalist roundly declared that misguided people must no longer go on applying the term "nigger" to a people capable of such great art as that shown by Indian ivories. Ivory carving might raise the status of the Indians, but it depressed that of the British

---

1. $3,040 at the modern rate of exchange.

125

sculptor craft worker, who felt himself unavailingly in competition with the cleverest people of the Far East. It was not just at the International Exhibition that this pre-eminence of the Eastern carver was felt, but on the domestic market in Britain generally. Who would buy one of Mr. Staight's ingenious chess sets, where all the white side were Crusaders, and all the red side Saracens, and all the castles straight from Viollet le Duc's book on medieval architecture, when by placing an order with a friend in the East India Company, he could have a "Company" set where all the pawns are Sepoys or Indian soldiers, the Kings are mounted on elephants, and the Bishops are mounted artillerymen on camels? Of course, the effects of Eastern competition on European ivory carvers is not purely an historic phenomenon. As has already been noticed, it is still felt by the ivory carvers of Dieppe.

In order to keep their heads above water in the face of apparently overwhelming competition, British ivory workers concentrated on just a few themes. The workmen and craft workers, as opposed to artists, carved very elaborate knife handles, hairbrushes, and other utilitarian objects that could not be so readily undertaken by Far Eastern workers, while the sculptors worked on the portrait bust and ultra miniature carvings.

Some of the most interesting ivories ever made were constructed in the last named art form by a group of artists who worked in Britain, although they have very European-sounding names —G. Stephany and Dresch, and Haager and Hess. The term "Voyez" ivories, which has been apparently incorrectly applied to this school of ivory carving, is really a very appropriate one because "Voyez," or "Behold," is just what Stephany or Dresch might have said when they showed you one of their ivories in their shop in Bath, or later on in London, where they became "Sculptors in Miniature to their Majesties King George the Third and Queen Charlotte." Their ivories are in fact peepshow scenes that have to be looked at really closely—peered at in effect— if they are going to achieve their full success. The sculptors obviously drew their inspiration from

theatrical scenery, although in reality most of their subjects are taken from out-of-doors. They include sea pieces, memorial plaques with pedestals, urns and mourners, and rural scenes. By means of incredibly delicate workmanship, the ivory is cut away from a slab perhaps half a centimeter thick so that it falls back in perspective, ending in a silhouette set against a background of opaque blue potglass. Perhaps this very unusual material was intended to suggest a night sky, with a scene illuminated by moonlight set against it. Although the medium is minute the effect is grandiose. Anyone looking into a snuffbox scene made by these sculptors can easily imagine himself walking across a forest glade, ringed with majestic trees, or approaching in awestruck reverence the portico of a great temple with a lofty pediment raised on soaring columns. To protect these carvings, the most fragile and delicate ever made, a glass shade was placed over the scene. This accentuates the hypnotic effect of the whole composition. Looking into a typical Stephany and Dresch plaque I can see a harbor, with a ship lying up, two ships under sail, a sail on the horizon, two boats (one with nine men in it and another with one), a crane, a warehouse, a fort with flags flying, and a distant sail on the horizon. I am almost afraid to go on looking, for fear the scene changes and another ship comes into port, or someone turns the corner of the sea wall. All this is achieved within the compass of about three and a half by one and a half inches.

Much more is known about the German Stephany, who was exhibiting ivory carvings at the Royal Academy from 1791 to 1803, than about any other member of the group. Artists of such distinction were obviously not at the start of their career, and the roots of miniature work of this sort must be sought in Europe. Voyez ivories have never received as much recognition in England as they deserve, but if there is one person who always appreciates a good ivory, it is another ivory carver. Stephany and Dresch's work became the foundation of much of the carving done in Dieppe, where many "medallions in bas relief silhouetted, and on blue glass, under a glass shade," to quote the catalogue of the Dieppe museum, can still be seen. So similar is a Voyez to a Dieppe ivory that the two can often be confused. Amongst the Stephany ivories in the Bristol collection, for instance, is one of a symbolic subject bearing a French inscription and signed "C. N.," initials that do not seem to represent any known British carver but may well be those of one of the prolific Nicolle family of Dieppe carvers.

There are important differences between the two schools. The Voyez ivories have the edges of the silhouettes pared away where they touch the blue glass until the ivory has become transparent and the blue can be seen coming through. Dieppe ivories on the other hand always give a solid appearance, even near to the edges. The flutes of the columns in classical buildings are cut out with a piercing saw at Dieppe, so that each flute shows blue against the white ground of the ivory column. In the Voyez ivories, each flute has been beautifully sculptured out, as if with Oberon's chisel. While the Stephany ivories have obviously been composed by someone with a painter's eye, as if for the drop scene in a theatre, with plenty of blue at the top of the picture to suggest the sky, in the Dieppe ivories the design has been decided on by someone who is obviously an ivory carver first and foremost. He has closed in the top of the composition whenever possible so as to avoid too much sky, often by bending the tops of trees in an alarming way so as to fill up the ground and waste as little ivory as possible. Often the blue is not kept for the sky background at all, but distributed here and there over the picture in a rather abstract way, so that on one Dieppe box a road is represented with ivory, the fields lying on either side of it by blue glass.

It was not just French carvers who were influenced by British ones; influence and inspiration could flow in the opposite direction. C. Kelly, who flourished around 1818, and William Ewing, whose active period was between 1829 and 1825, both made profiles in high relief,

Bust of a woman, by English carver C. Kelly, 1818. (Victoria and Albert Museum, London)

which obviously owe something to similar portrait half busts made in Dieppe.

Queen Victoria was too busy admiring some groups of stuffed frogs from Wurtemberg dressed in human clothing and arranged in life-like groups (one of them was shaving another) to admire the ivories of Charles Cockle Lucas at the Great Exhibition of 1851. Lucas, who died in 1883 at 83, had begun life working as a cutler at Winchester. He progressed from carving ivory knife handles to sculpturing heads in ivory. The indifference shown by the Queen to the ivory carvings on show at the Crystal Palace was shared by the press, although praise was lavished on the ivory architectural models in the Fine Art Court on the "pretty turned ivory and wooden snuffboxes of Mr. Garrett of Ipswich" and on a "candlestick in wood and ivory by W. D. Kemphill, M.D." The last exhibit was in fact a danger signal. It was one of what a Victorian author called "those extraordinary productions of skill and taste that come from the hands of the amateur turner, who uses for the production of a fragile gewgaw tools and appliances that only affluence can afford."

Turning ivory on a lathe specially constructed to give all sorts of unusual effects had been popular with many amateurs—including kings and princes—in Europe during the 17th and 18th centuries. Its popularity in Britain, however, may be said to date from the publication of Charles Holtzapfel's book, *Turning and Mechanical Manipulation,* in 1847. Holtzapfel obviously knew a lot about ivory (his recipe for bleaching the material by exposing it to sunlight under a glass

Ivory Chessmen, turned by Charles Holtzapfel. Although Holtzapfel claimed that he made all his work completely on the lathe, one cannot help feeling that he must have used a chisel here and there just to trim up the finished product. (Science Museum, London)

Benjamin Cheverton's sculpturing machine, 1826. This English inventor's machine enabled copies on a reduced scale to be made of larger-sized busts. Motion was applied to the rotary files, which did the rough carving; the sculpture was then finished by hand. (Science Museum, London)

Queen Victoria. Bust by Benjamin Cheverton.
(Victoria and Albert Museum, London)

shade is just as effective now as it was when he invented it). Unfortunately for ivory carving, he explained to his readers how they could form ivory into the most ingenious shapes by machinery on the special lathe he designed for himself—not by hand with a carving tool. Holzapfel would have been extremely popular nowadays because all his carvings were in effect abstract or figurative designs, and thus extremely modern. It is at least possible to suggest, however, that every time an ivory turner is made an ivory carver is spoiled, and a lot of potential creative artists must have been spoiled as Victorians took up Holtzapfel's attractive but purely mechanical hobby.

Also prominent at the Great Exhibition of 1851 was the Cheverton Reducing Machine. Benjamin Cheverton, who died in 1876 at about 82, had invented a device in 1828 that could make identically sized copies or small-sized copies of full-scale busts or plaques. Because the sections of ivory from which he would carve the copy were always smaller than the original bust, his ivory heads are usually fairly small. Cheverton apparently made more busts than plaques, and his finished work is signed with his own name as well as that of the original artist. His carvings have been meticulously worked over so that no sign of the activity of his reducing machine (which was a sort of pointing machine with rotary cutters) remains. His delightful pocket-sized replicas look so much better than his originals that he must have been a dangerous rival to sculptors like Lucas who carved ivory directly.

But although ivory turning and Cheverton busts are charming, their effect was to still further depress the status of the English ivory carver. To many heedless people, ivory became associated with a sort of artisanal craft work—like meerschaum for meerschaum pipes. If you wanted an artistic ivory, you would have to go to the Far East. The report by the correspondent of the *Illustrated London News* of the International Exhibition of 1862 exemplifies this attitude. It discusses the use of ivory for turning,

"Cupid Breaking His Bow," by English sculptor Richard Cockle Lucas, 1800–1883. (Victoria and Albert Museum, London)

hair brushes, billiard balls, umbrella handles, and so forth, and then concludes: "Of course the Indian and Chinese Courts showed the most elaborate work of the carver in ivory."

The year 1862 marked the acquisition by the Victoria and Albert Museum in London, which had been founded with the proceeds of the Great Exhibition of 1851, of the most important studio ivory that had yet been seen in England. It was a vase that had been made two years before by a distinguished visiting sculptor.

"Bacchus," by Baron Henri de Triqueti. (British Museum, London)

The first complete photographic record (pages 133–137) to be published of Baron Henri de Triqueti's monumental vase (formerly in the Victoria and Albert Museum, London). This work by the naturalized French Piedmontese sculptor emphasizes the close connection that has always existed between literature and ivory sculpture. The whole vase is, as it were, an act of homage to the famous poets of antiquity. (Victoria and Albert Museum, London)

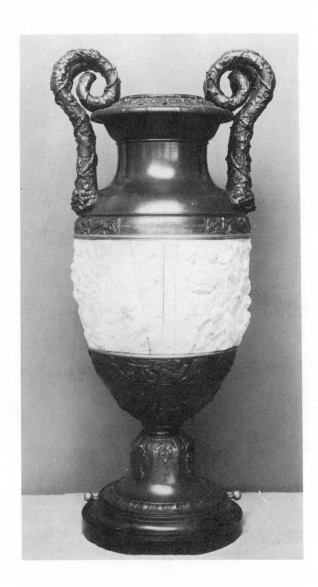

Baron Henri de Triqueti was a Piedmontese whose speciality was decorating royal tombs. He had made the sculptures for a cenotaph to the Duke of Orleans, one of the claimants to the throne of France. This had been followed by another, and much more important, royal commission, to carve reliefs inside the memorial chapel to Queen Victoria's consort, Prince Albert, at Windsor Castle. De Triqueti's fame as an ivory carver must have been on a par with his achievements in the field of memorial sculpture, because the British Museum in London had already acquired one of his ivory statues, "Bacchus," by 1859. The Triqueti vase is a combination of bronze and ivory. This use of two or more materials suggests strongly that it was Triqueti who acted as the bridge between pure ivory sculpture, such as his "Bacchus," which had characterized the start of the century, and the ivory and metal sculpture, which was going to end it. Although there were other competitors for the honor of having begun combination sculpture, such as Simart, for example, who could claim to have worked in two materials at once, these materials had been ivory and gold or ivory and gilded silver. A composition vase in ivory and bronze is rather different from a statue in chryselephantine work because it has not been suggested by a reading of the classics, nor does it owe its origin to attempts at a revival of chryselephantine statuary such as were made by antiquaries like Quatremère de Quincy. The Triqueti vase is therefore a bridging piece.

It is very difficult to criticize this work, not least of all because the Victoria and Albert repented of its enthusiasm for modern ivories in 1956, and a Board of Survey condemned it as "unsuitable" and sold it to an unknown purchaser. The photographic record (such as it is) of the vase is set before the reader in the illustrations; it is obviously inadequate in that it does not provide a clear indication as to what the inscriptions are about. Nevertheless, they obviously occupy a large and integral part in the composition. In spite of the photographs it is possible to see that de Triqueti has combined two

styles, the classical representationalism that is so characteristic of the massive goblets and plates made by Otto Glenz, and the work of the decoratives that was to be so strongly influenced by literary romanticism. So the vase looks backward to the massive Borghese and Medici vases made by Blard in Dieppe in 1833, and forward to the composite bronze and ivory sculpture associated with a man who was now to step into the never-ending task of completing the memorial work in the Albert Chapel, Sir Alfred Gilbert.

Although with many artists it is merely an affectation, there is such a thing as the artistic temperament. Gilbert's artistic integrity nearly destroyed him; he lost his money, his friends, and his royal patrons, and he even had to resign from the Royal Academy, membership of which in Victorian times was lucrative as well as honorable. The suite of rooms in Windsor Castle that had been offered to him when he had gone bankrupt was withdrawn, and finally he was branded as a criminal because he was supposed to have abstracted some of the figures that he had already made, at Queen Victoria's request, for the tomb of the Duke of Clarence, and sold them to other patrons surreptitiously.

All his troubles arose from the fact that he was never satisfied with anything he had made. He had to begin making it all over again, to the exasperation of his patrons, who felt their time and money were being wasted. Gilbert's dissatisfaction with what he did was incomprehensible to everyone except himself. The master merely had to pick up a piece of lead foil which had wrapped up an ounce of tobacco and twist it into shape for bystanders to perceive he was a great sculptor. In fact the main difference between Gilbert and Benvenuto Cellini, with whom, because of their stormy lives, he has often been compared, was that Cellini was always pleased with what he had done, Gilbert never.

Like Cellini, Gilbert was just as much a goldsmith as a sculptor. In fact it was from the Florentine Renaissance that Gilbert drew most of his inspiration, so it is not surprising to find him producing works that, like those of the

Another figure from the same frieze, showing the "direct glance" of Lynn Jenkins's figures as opposed to the "downcast glance" of Gilbert and his followers.

Renaissance, are made from many different materials worked into a unified composition. Gilbert was obviously influenced by the Belgian Revival as well. He became an associate of the Royal Academy in 1887, the year of the Brussels Exhibition, which marks the rise of combination sculpture in Europe, and he may have noted the existence of earlier combination pieces, such as the "Ceres" in ivory and bronze shown at the International Exhibition in 1871 and afterwards purchased by the Bethnal Green Museum, London.

Gilbert, however, united so many diverse influences—he had spent long periods in Paris and Rome as well as Florence, and lived for a time at Bruges—and had so much originality that he soon founded his own school of sculpture—the Decorative Movement. The materials used by the Decoratives—onyx, turquoise and turquoise matrix, moonstone, aquamarine, rubies, sapphires, beryls, and emeralds—sound like the names of the heroines in a Dante Gabriel Rossetti poem. The same debt to the contemporary English Pre-Raphaelite literary movement is apparent in the titles of the works of Gilbert and his followers. The American sculptor W. Reynolds Stephens, for example, who was a particularly gifted disciple of Gilbert's, was very fond of using subjects from Arthurian legends, such as Guinevere and Lancelot. The subjects were not treated realistically (if, that is, a realistic treatment of a legend is possible) but were dressed in extraordinary clothes, unrelated to any period or place in real life. Gilbert's treatment of the armor of his figures is particularly original and interesting, based as it is on his study of shells. We are only concerned with the faces and hands of his figures, because they were the only parts of the sculpture that were made of ivory. Here the influence that he had on his followers can clearly be seen, because they all, with the exception of Lynn Jenkins, copied Gilbert in giving their figures a downcast glance, like that which first appears in the ivory face of the St. George, which Gilbert made for an épergne to be presented to Queen Victoria by the officers of her regiments. The eyes of the Jenkins figures on the great frieze that I will mention in a moment regard the onlooker with a candid charm, those of all the other Decoratives have a downcast glance that adds considerably to the air of mystery which this school loved to infuse into its work.

The subjects of the Decorative School, figures who appeared to be wandering through a glade in Camelot, were inseparably connected with the materials used. The bright polychrome decorative stones and the use of Japanese metal patination techniques evoked the Middle Ages of romance as much as did, say, Lynn Jenkin's figure of the good knight Sir Lancelot cradling a waif whom he has taken under his protection in his mail-clad arms. It was as a contrast to the green bronze draperies and bright metal enrichments of his figures that Gilbert had adopted yellow, mellowed ivory for their hands and faces, because it offered such a splendid contrast. Unlike many contemporary sculptors, he apparently felt ivory was so important that he worked it himself, disdaining the services of a journeyman ivory carver or *practicien*.

When a commission came from Windsor Castle, the nearest thing England has to Camelot, to decorate the tomb of Queen Victoria's grandson, the Duke of Clarence, Gilbert could hardly refuse. The length of time it took to carve the ivory faces and hands of the figures that were put in place and those that were afterwards abandoned may have contributed to the disastrous delays that were to bring upon Gilbert royal displeasure, ruin, and self-imposed exile. By the time the tomb was finally finished, in 1928, it was a monument to Decorative Sculpture as well as to the Duke of Clarence. Gilbert had stopped working in that style by then, and so had everyone else.

While it lasted the Decorative School had contributed many memorable works to English sculpture, such as the "Lamia" by George Frampton, in whose work ivory plays an even larger part than it had in Gilbert's. Frampton was an avowed rebel against "white" sculpture in marble, and this shows that ivory was now valued for its ability to take on a yellow, aged tone, just the very quality for which it had been criticized by Bernardin de St. Pierre a hundred years before.

The revolt against whiteness could not have been taken much further than in the work of Reynolds Stephens. This Detroit-born sculptor, who was later knighted for his services to art, was also a metalworker, a marble worker, an enameler, and a painter. His works glow with the color of reflecting gems, as do those of his contemporary, Frank Lynn Jenkins. Jenkins is of particular interest in that one of his major works is permanently on view—a frieze 80 feet long, of bronze, ivory, and mother-of-pearl—in

Sir Alfred Gilbert. "The Virgin with Roses" (sometimes described as "St. Elizabeth of Hungary"). Figure for the Duke of Clarence's tomb, Albert Memorial Chapel, Windsor Castle, England. (Reproduced by gracious permission of Her Majesty the Queen)

Frieze in ivory, mother-of-pearl, and bronze for Lloyd's Shipping Registry, by Frank Lynn Jenkins. This frieze, at 71 Fenchurch Street, London, can be seen by request and is one of the few important pieces of combination sculpture still viewable. Exhibited in the Royal Academy, 1901. Note the disappearance of the original joining collar that connected the ivory neck and the bronze dress.

Lloyd's Registry of Shipping on Fenchurch Street, London. All too often the works of ivory sculptors of the Decorative School can only be seen from photographs, sometimes not taken from the original, which have, consequently, lost some of their appeal. Many of them appear to be lost for good, others have disappeared into the limbo of semi-public collections, such as the Chantrey Bequest in London, which holds the marble and ivory "Pandora" of Harry Bates.

The impressions made by a pilgrimage to Fenchurch Street to see Lynn Jenkins' frieze are bound to be mixed. The figures reveal both the strengths and the weaknesses of Decorative Sculpture. It is impossible not to admire the force and daring of the composition, which shows the fantasy of the school at its best; yet the frieze, which once glowed with color, now looks rather drab. The mother-of-pearl panels have gone "blind" as mother-of-pearl always will if exposed constantly to the light.* This suggests that one of the mistakes made by the Decoratives was experimenting with materials whose lasting effects had not been properly assessed. The bronzes are also a hue that is probably different from what the sculptor intended—the effects of the London atmosphere on bronze are striking and of course of more than aesthetic interest to those who must breathe it. The present condition of the frieze also underlines the fact that the weakness of a combination sculpture is the place where the two materials meet. One of the figures has lost its ivory hands, wrenched off during the war, and a bronze collar is gone from the neck of another. "A vessel all in silver and gold," Dunstan Pruden told me "is more enduring and foolproof than something that has to be screwed or otherwise joined together. I used to employ semi-precious stones quite a lot with silver, but I have tended more and more to discontinue the practice, as it makes the object less organic."

A similar consideration may have entered the

minds of the Decoratives as the 20th century approached. Making combination sculpture was rather like juggling with a number of balls at once; it was easy for one of them to drop—for one substance not to be effectively worked—and then the whole effect was spoiled. Moreover, as Alfred Maskell pointed out, it took a master hand to achieve harmony in a composition that could easily begin to appear vulgar, sensuous, and claptrap.

As a reaction against Combination Sculpture, and the kind of sculpture that was made by handing a plaster model to an apprentice and telling him to copy it with the pointing machine in marble, a school of Direct Carving now began to appear. Because the Direct Carvers believed in doing all their work themselves, sculpting their own marble and wood and so forth, they were in effect limiting themselves to work in one material at a time. It was impossible for any one sculptor to handle all the materials used in a piece of combination sculpture; he would, for example, rely on a lapidary to shape the turquoises he would add to a decorative frieze. The Direct Carvers were often strongly influenced by the Arts and Crafts Movement. They wanted to enhance the status of the craftsman and could see nothing wrong with making, say, an ivory paperknife, whereas sculptors of the earlier part of the century might have felt this was below their dignity.

The turning point between combination sculpture in ivory and direct sculpture is to be seen in the work of Richard Garbe, who began exhibiting in 1898. It is even possible to point to one of his works, "Primavera," which is a compromise between the combination and the direct style. In "Primavera" gilt is used in combination with Ivory. The central figure stands in a niche against an architectural background that would not look out of place in one of Frampton's sculptures. Primavera herself, however, is cut from a whole tusk, in an extremely naturalistic pose that was probably suggested by the tusk's curving lines. She could be removed from her background and exhibited separately without sacri-

---

* For more discussion of this condition of mother-of-pearl see *Carving Shells and Cameos*, Carson I. A. Ritchie, London, 1970.

Head, by Richard Garbe. Although confined scrupulously to the limits imposed by a block of ivory, this head, like so many of Garbe's works, conveys an impression of complete freedom. The wind-blown hair, waving foliage, and tumbling waves—which are features of many of Garbe's carvings—help to contribute to this impression of abandon.

though blown into place by a gentle breeze. This was a revolutionary return to the practice of the Middle Ages, when sculptors of the Romanesque period had carved swaying Virgins so as to use up the whole of the tusk and thus avoid carpentering together bits of ivory in what might prove to be an unsound job. "I have carved figures that conformed to the curves of the tusk," wrote Garbe, "and as these lines are in themselves expressive and fine, I have incorporated them into the composition. I have a strong sentimental and economic appreciation of ivory, and abhor wasting it to no purpose. But as an enforced emphasis on the tusk shape would unduly limit the use of that material, I have no compunction in cutting a tusk into slabs for the purpose of reliefs or other designs."

Garbe was to exert a considerable influence

ficing the effect of the work.

Although Garbe was a very talented sculptor who deliberately tried to diversify his work as much as possible, the kind of Garbe carving that would be used to illustrate his style by someone writing about his work or by a fellow sculptor who was trying to absorb what he had to teach would probably be a tusk-sized female figure, often nude, sometimes surrounded by streaming drapery or foliage, and always swaying gracefully to meet the natural curve of the ivory as

Head, by Richard Garbe.

his friends told me. The effects of his impact on ivory carving have even now not been fully worked out. Ivory carving in England today is miniature rather that monumental, because it is difficult to get a very large statue out of just one tusk, if it was not to be used in combination with other materials. To a certain extent the status of the ivory carver shrank with his works. He began to gravitate toward the Royal Society of Miniature Artists (housed for a long time at an address

"Dryad of the Willows," by Richard Garbe, 1949.

"Aurora," by Richard Garbe, 1948. Although this is a late work, it displays the characteristic swaying figure that fills the whole curve of the tusk and that is typical of much of the sculptor's early, as well as late, work.

on ivory carving by his position as Professor at the Central School of Arts and Crafts, by the length of his career, and by the charm of his personality; "He was a perfect darling" one of

that appropriately enough, is half a street number[2]) rather than the Royal Academy of Arts.
Largely because they had become smaller and
were unlikely to enter into an important composition, such as Gilbert's tomb for the Duke of
Clarence, ivories began to attract less notice from
critics and public.

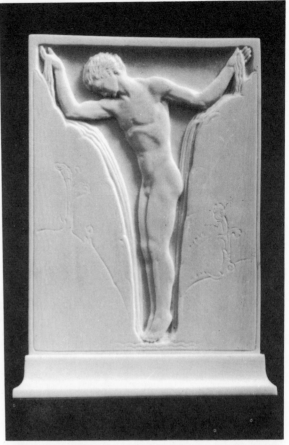

"The Source," by Richard Garbe, 1951. Garbe
was just as much a master of the bas-relief as of
a carving in the natural shape of the tusk.

Figure, by Richard Garbe. Note how the design
fits within the confines of a naturally shaped
block of ivory, in this case the tip of the tusk.

These changes were still in the future, the
effect of Garbe on his pupils and admirers was
more immediate. Jeanne Bell found him an in-
spiring teacher at the Central School of Arts and
Crafts. "He was always very kind to me, and
interested in my work, though he said I was
'too independent for him,' because I would not
let him work himself on anything I was doing.
He liked to take a tool and work on things
himself and at the Central School most of his
students were only too pleased for him to help
them in this way. He believed very strongly in
doing most of the work with the chisel and
scraper, and using files as little as possible. As
a sculptor he advised me to concentrate on the
figure, human or animal, and to do only what

_____
2. 6½ Suffolk Street, Pall Mall East, London W1. It has
now moved to the Mall.

"Pastoral," by Jeanne Bell, 1949.

I could ask a good price for." In spite of Jeanne Bell's independence, I feel some influence of Garbe can be detected in her "Daphne," in which the figure's hand, raised above its head and disappearing in foliage, recalls that of Garbe's "Dryad."

Alan Durst was another pupil of Garbe's. The youngest of the large family of a Canon of Winchester, he wanted to become a sculptor immediately, but his father urged him to try something else first. He served as an officer in the Royal Marines, but his attention was redirected back to art by a chance visit to the Tate Gallery with his brother. The latter criticized a statue of Hamlet, Garbe objected that it was well carved. "Good heavens," was the reply, "you don't think sculptors do their own carving do you?" His brother explained how the sculptor would simply hand his *practicien* a model, from which the latter would carve the stone with the help of a pointing machine. Then and there Durst decided that he would devote himself to some art that *had* to be done by hand. He chose stained glass, and began studying design and ivory carving under Garbe. A period of artistic indigestion set in, and he decided to go to Chartres for a year and study the windows there.

During his stay at Chartres he found he was spending more time looking at the statues on the front than at the glass. He was still looking at them when the postman climbed the steps to hand him his recall to the Royal Marines. World War I was about to break out. Within two days he was at sea in a battleship; now he no longer had any statues to look at so he had to start carving. At the West African ports where his ship touched, ivory and ebony lay stacked up on the quayside, with no shipping to take them away because of the German submarines. In between directing the gunfire of his battery, Alan Durst began carving seriously, greatly to the interest of his fellow officers.

Perhaps the strongest link between Garbe and Durst is the latter's delightful animals, some of the most charming ever made in ivory. Alan Durst had the knack of impressing his person-

"Bear," by Alan Durst.

ality on whatever he made, whether it was a monumental statue for the front of a cathedral or a charming *bibelot,* such as the ivory and ebony box (a wedding present for his wife) he showed me in his lovely studio home at Hampstead.

Works such as these are the product of considerable leisure, and leisure was one of the casualties of the first World War. When a new generation of sculptors began work after the war, they were sometimes so pressed for time that they carved ivory on trains and buses.

"Eric Gill carved no ivory when I was with

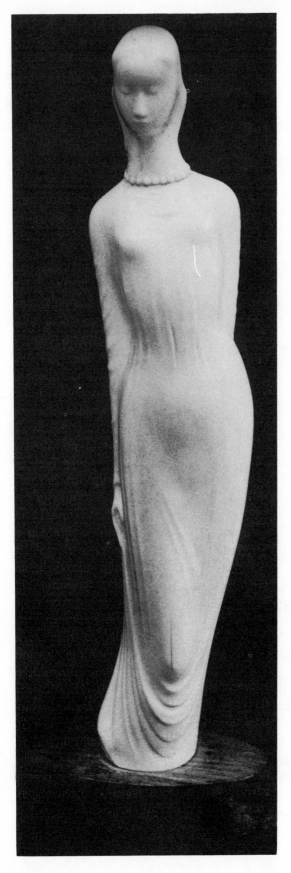

Figure, by Donald Potter.

him," recalls his pupil, Donald Potter, who is himself a distinguished ivory sculptor. "He was too busy earning money to pay off his mortgage on Pigotts, where he lived. Laurie Cribb, his lettering assistant, told me he used to get bits of ivory given him that he carved. This particular walrus tooth was done while he was living in the Welsh mountains at Llanthony Abbey. He got so fascinated with it that he finished it off on a train journey to London and back! Potter continues: "I enclose a very old photo (see line drawing) of one of his ivories that I know very little about, never having seen it . . . I think it was exhibited in his first exhibition at the Goupil Gallery in the 1920s, and was bought by a priest (Father Brown, not his real name, who crops up in G. K. Chesterton's detective books, and was taken from real life, he was a friend of Gill's)."

Philip Hagreen, also a friend of Eric Gill's, was another ivory sculptor. He had evolved a new method of ivory carving, the scraper method, based on the techniques of Far Eastern carvers, and he was to pass it on to Dunstan Pruden, who will describe it later.

Another commuter ivory sculptor was Everatt Gray. He had broken into ivory carving through sculpture in wood, and like so many 20th-century ivory carvers, had taught himself. Ivory was a very convenient medium, because, as Mrs. Gray says, "It could be done in his armchair in the evenings, or on a train, or on the top of a red London bus to and from his office in Kew Gardens. During those bus journeys his work created a certain amount of interest in the conductors, producing such comments as 'clever old stick, aren't you?' and sometimes complaints about the ivory dust on the floor, whilst school girls breathed heavily down the back of his neck. He was very meticulous not only in the carving, but also in the polishing of the finished article, for which he used chiefly putty powder with pieces of old silk. We had little money but in those days one could often find tusks in old junk shops and sometimes old billiard balls became waterlilies."

Everatt Gray is an ivory sculptor to whom

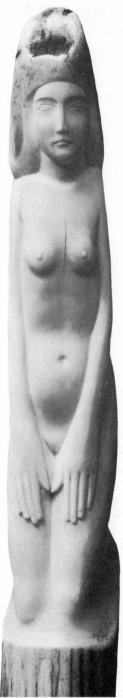

"Figure," by Eric Gill. (Victoria and Albert Museum, London)

many. Other undervalued sculptors who would take a large place in this gallery if it existed are Mary Morton, Associate of the Royal Society of British Sculptors in 1928, who succeeded better than anyone else in remaining purely representational while using the whole surface that the shape of the tusk offered; Arthur George Walker, who made ivory heads on bases of green Connemara marble and ivory drinking cups ornamented by a frieze of bacchanals, another example of a carver waiting for re-assessment; and William Simmonds, who exhibited some charming ivories at the Alpine Club Gallery in 1921.

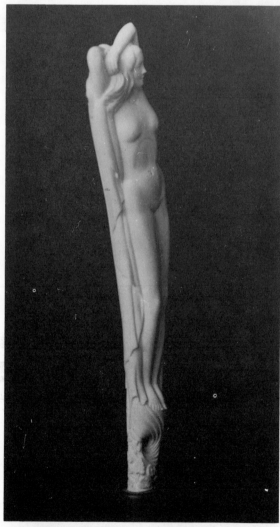

"Convallaria," by W. Everatt Gray, 1949. Note the influence of Richard Garbe.

insufficient attention has been paid in the past, largely because we have no art gallery devoted only to ivory sculptures such as exists in Ger-

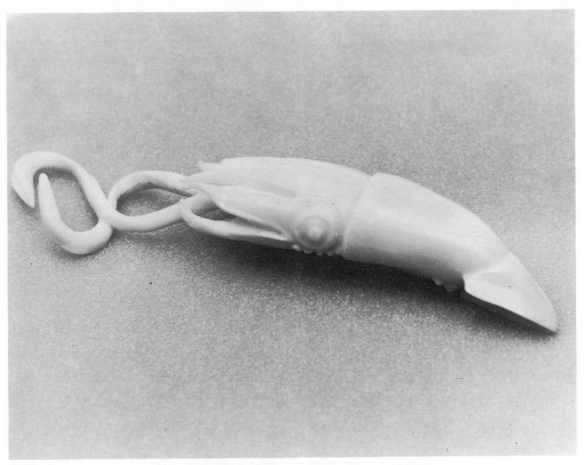

"Deep Sea Squid," by W. Everatt Gray. Carved from a whale's tooth.

Ivory carving has never woven such close connections with the church in this country as it has in say Austria, where the occupation of *bildhauer,* or "image hewer," in ivory or wood is a recognized and respected one. There are church workers in ivory: Alan Durst; Donald Potter, who taught himself to carve ("I've carved most of my life, taking to it naturally in my early youth with no teaching"); and Joyce Bidder, another autodidact ("I took to ivory as a medium by happening one day on my grandfather's set of ivory rules and scales—he was a civil engineer. They cut into very nice paper knives with low relief carving, and polished beautifully."

Even the dedicated religious carver who belongs to some such organization as the Society of Church Craftsmen or the Society of Catholic Sculptors is much more likely to turn his chisel toward secular rather than religious work. One of our greatest religious sculptors aptly likened the amount of church commissions the average artist will receive, as compared with his lay work, to the tip of an iceberg. Ivories are difficult to display in churches because of their small size and also the difficulties of insurance. A rector or vicar who buys a statue of the Virgin is much more likely to keep it in his study than display it in the church. Great numbers of patrons of works that are to appear in churches want a monument to a loved relative or friend more than anything else, and ivories do not lend themselves

Mary Morton's "Nature's Tribute to Beauty,"
1935.

mittees, can provide more difficulties for the
sculptor than any lay commission because the
committee keeps changing its mind. Because so
much English ivory work has been religious,
especially during the Middle Ages, it is fitting
to take our leave of it by looking at the work
of a man whose carvings would have been ap-

to memorial work. Artists rarely refuse commissions on the grounds that they themselves
have no religious beliefs (it would be impossible
to decorate any church nowadays if it were only
done by the faithful, and the creative spirit in
man obviously derives from God the Creator
whether an artist is a Christian or not). Some
artists, however, find that church patronage,
which is usually nowadays administered by com-

Another view of "Nature's Tribute to Beauty."

Another view of the same. Great technical virtuosity has been shown in the way in which the design is made to fit into the natural cylinder of the tusk.

preciated by that great church patron and first of English ivory collectors, Alfred the Great.

Dunstan Pruden is perhaps best known as an ivory carver from his "Buckfast Crozier," made from mammoth ivory. Like so many other ivory carvers he is a goldsmith, and his work in metals

has helped him to create exactly the right tools he wants—silver steel scrapers, tempered to a pale straw color in the fire and then forged to pencil size. These tiny tools enable him to take off a tiny sliver of ivory with each stroke and build up the intricate work for which he is known. The scraper leaves a polished surface on which one can draw with a pencil at any stage of the carving and which requires little treatment afterwards. What a pity that such a fine carver should have virtually stopped carving! He himself provides the explanation: "I did quite a bit of ivory carving at one time, but because I am primarily a goldsmith, my clients don't leave me any leisure for it any more. Scarely any other craftsmen in precious metals do figurative work today, so I find that this takes up all my time."

Again and again this word "leisure" has been mentioned in my talks with contemporary ivory carvers. Ivory carving is slow, it cannot be hurried. But the sculptor is, after all, working for his living. He cannot refuse a lucrative commission that he can complete in a few days in order to spend months fashioning a work which he must, in the end, sell for a good deal less than it cost him to make. There is no doubt that British sculptors will always go on making ivories, just for the love of them. This love is partly inspired by a fondness for the material, partly by contact with other carvers. Richard Robertson of Aberdeen, for example, owes his primary inspiration to his studies under Thomas Bayliss Huxley Jones. However, as no formal instruction in ivory is given in England any more, there is no hope of this master-pupil relationship continuing into the future. Young sculptors are unlikely to become inspired just by the sight of an ivory, as Pierre Graillon was, because they never see them. Ivories are representational and consequently banned from most London galleries. They are only to be seen in two regularly exhibiting societies, the Royal Academy of Arts and the Royal Society of Miniature Painters, Sculptors, and Gravers. In a few years time, if present trends continue, the ivory carver will either be extinct or will have become a very rare

Medallions for an Altar Cross, by Alan Durst.
Alan Durst's religious carvings range between
the monumental and the miniature.

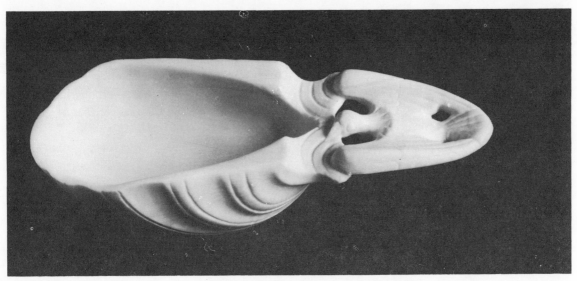

"Liturgical Shell," by Alan Durst.

species indeed, like the cameo carver, instead of taking a prominent place in the arts.

Is there any way out of the present crisis of the ivory sculptor in Britain? Several steps might be taken which, if they did not revivify ivory carving, would at least ensure that it did not perish unsuccored. Formal instruction in ivory carving should be reintroduced into at least one art college in Britain. "Real carvers are getting scarcer and rarer," comments Donald Potter. "The Art Schools are doing so little towards training the young—they are much too busy with their facile plaster work and what they call 'constructions' that they have no time or skilled teachers for carving. That was one of the valuable things about being with Eric Gill; he was, amongst other things, a superb craftsman." A collection of modern ivories should ·be formed in London and put on permanent display. At present our biggest gallery of modern art, the Tate, only houses one modern ivory and it can only be seen by appointment. Prizes ought to be offered for ivory carving, and some fraction of larger art commissions diverted to ivory sculptors. Ivory merchants are unlikely ever to make any money by selling ivory to sculptors, because sculptors use very little. When I mentioned the name of Dunstan Pruden to Frederick Friedlein he had first to consult with one of his oldest em-

Madonna carved in a walrus tooth (on the train), by Eric Gill.

ployees and finally to turn up the books to discover when he had last sold a tusk to Pruden. All ivory merchants, however, love their stock in trade and respect it as the raw material of fine craftsmanship. They could testify to their admiration by donating tusks to ivory sculptors, as the Belgian government did, even if they were only the tusks that were so badly damaged that they were no longer usable by the makers of piano keys and hairbrushes—the principal customers for ivory in Britain.

Chapter 8.

Collecting Modern Ivories

The collector of modern ivories enjoys many advantages over someone who has decided to collect those of an earlier period. For one thing, he will know that he is getting what he paid for. When I mentioned to Mr. Charles Avery of the Victoria and Albert Museum, London, that I was writing a history of modern ivory carvers, he enquired: "Do you mean the people who make 20th-century medieval statues? If so, you'll find plenty of them." Ivory fakers have almost as long a tradition to look back on as ivory carvers. We have already seen how one Dieppe carver, Perrin, moved to Paris to start a factory for making "medieval" ivories and "aging" them by boiling them in tea. Another method used by 19th-century dealers to give their statuettes a medieval patina was to make their wives hang them on a chain around their neck between their breasts. There is nothing to stop any unscrupulous dealer from doing the same thing today, even though dealers' wives, like other women, no longer seem to be cast in the mold of Victorian females. Medieval ivories were fairly stereotyped in design, and consequently fairly easy to imitate. Carbon dating tests are not likely to be of much use in assessing their age, as they could easily be made from mammoth ivory.

It is a very different business to fake a modern ivory. In the first place the styles that the moderns use are much more individual. Before faking, for example, a Richard Garbe, a modern carver would have to acquire his technique; he would have to be careful not to release too many pseudo Richard Garbe carvings on the market, so by the time he had done one or two he would have to move on to another sculptor and imitate *his* style. It would be a time-consuming business and not worth the trouble, because for the same amount of effort he could have carved several "medieval" Virgins that would fetch much more. Moreover, modern ivories are sold so cheaply that they do not really pay the sculptors for the work they put in them. They offer a margin of profit much less than the average faker would demand.

Of course this is one of the other big attractions about modern ivories—they are relatively inexpensive. Nothing that occupies a sculptor for several months will be cheaply priced, but a carving by one of the first masters costs less than an easel painting by an artist of comparative distinction. Whereas smaller bibelots can be bought for less, a tusk figure or group will sell for about $300. At this price it is possible to form a really representative collection of all the living British ivory sculptors or a group of works to show the development of style in one particular carver. It is even possible to go below the normal buying price if a policy of selective buying is maintained. Several considerations will ensure that an ivory carving sells cheaply; it may have been damaged,

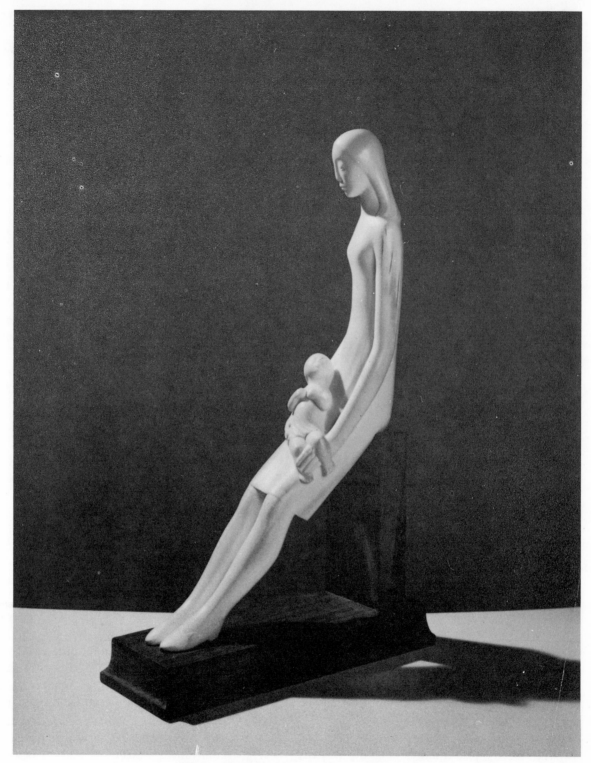

"Girl with Baby," by Gwynneth Holt.

and although the damage need have been no more than minimal, it will still affect the price. Gwynneth Holt told me about one of her statues that had been cracked by being exhibited too close to a high-powered electric light bulb. Reluctantly she had to let it go for much less than it was worth. Sculptures made by a carver at the beginning of his career, and still unsold toward the end if it, will have dropped in price owing to the effect of inflation, while perhaps a still lower price can be negotiated because sculptors tend to tire of work that hangs on their hands too long. As a general rule, the work of sculptors recently dead will sell fairly cheaply. Widows and other surviving relatives are often much less concerned about the price of a carving than that it should find an honored home in some important or private collection. It is always better to buy the work of a sculptor whose work has not received sufficient acclaim in the hope that his stock will rise, rather than that of someone whose popularity is at its height, in the hope that it will continue unchanged. "I was friendless, and ye took me in," is the sort of text that collectors should hang on their walls. Everatt Gray, for example, was considered much less *avant garde* than Gwynneth Holt. His carvings could have been acquired, during the period in which they were regarded as unfashionable, for very much less than will have to be paid for them a few years hence.

To a certain extent this advice will have been wasted in that many people who want to buy the ivories of a particular sculptor, such as Richard Garbe, do so because they have admired his work in other media and feel that while they may never be able to acquire one of his larger works in stone they could, by pinching themselves, buy an ivory.

Although the greatest bargains are undoubtedly to be obtained by buying 20th-century ivories, many people feel drawn toward some particular kind of ivory that is often an antique, such as a Cheverton bust. They feel they would like to acquire some American scrimshaw in England and take it back to its country of origin,

or perhaps they dream of acquiring an American ship model. The first rule in collecting is to collect what you like; the second is to like what you have collected. Interest in a collection will be maintained at its highest if each item is documented as much as possible. Every piece in a collection should be given an inconspicuous number written in india ink on the base with a mapping pen. This number should be entered in a catalogue, which ought to contain the date of acquisition, the price paid, the type of ivory used, the signature or other identification of the sculptor, and the past history of the piece. The collector should try to learn as much as possible about the work of the artists represented in his collection. This information is best kept in a separate book. If you collect modern ivories, write to the sculptor who carved each item and try to get as much information from him about it as you can. If you have any particularly interesting pieces, 17th-century scrimshaw for example, interest art historians in them, or better still, publish them yourself. Try to see as many collections of ivory as possible. In America there are those of Mr. Norbert Beihoff, the late Dr. S. A. Schneidmann, and the Milwaukee Museum; in Europe the Erbacher Elfenbeinmuseum, Otto-Glenz Strasse 1, Erbach, Odenwald, Germany, and the Musée de Dieppe, the Chateau, Dieppe, Seine Inferieure, France, are easily the best. Nobody who is interested in American scrimshaw should omit a visit to the Museum of Fisheries, Hull, England, and the Scott Polar Research Institute, Cambridge, England. Other British museums contain scrimshaw but they are too numerous to mention here.

Maintaining ivories in good condition is not a difficult task, after all ivory is the only organic material to come down to us in good condition from the last ice age. Like wood, ivory contains a great deal of water. It is very susceptible to sudden changes of temperature. A block of soft African ivory that I left in a centrally heated study cracked in a spiral pattern. Cracks, however, often close up again. Raw ivory tusks are kept in special cellar-like store rooms partly be-

American Collector and Treasures. The late Dr.
S. A. Schneidmann holding a Gwynneth Holt
ivory.

low ground; they are unheated, so that in winter
the warehousemen have to wear thickly lined
coats. Although the temperature inside the warehouse rarely reaches freezing point, it seems safer
to store raw ivory in a colder rather than warmer
place.

This consideration does not apply so forcefully

to ivory carvings, which have lost some of their
water content and appear to be more robust than
tusks, as they survive exhibition in heated galleries without warping or cracking, although of
course they are protected by being enclosed in a
fairly air-tight glass case. No ivory should ever
be kept near a direct source of heat, such as a

light bulb or radiator, or else it may crack. Otherwise, ivories can safely be kept at a temperature and humidity suitable for wooden objects. At an ordinary room temperature, between 60° and 70°F., a moisture content corresponding to 55 percent relative humidity would be in order. A fall of 10 percent in the humidity would not be disastrous for ivory carvings, but anything below that could be considered dangerous. Ivory sculptures, which are usually either carvings in the round or bas reliefs, will withstand temporary falls of relative humidity, even of a drastic nature, whereas pieces of thin ivory, such as the base for an ivory miniature portrait, are far more vulnerable and will react immediately to atmospheric variations.

The spot where an ivory is displayed in a room deserves a good deal of thought. If in a cabinet, it is relatively safe, provided the cabinet is not near a radiator or a door. If it is on an open bracket, it should certainly be placed above the reach of dogs or children. Jeanne Bell gives a warning on this subject: "I am often asked what is the cause of ivory becoming rather yellow and discolored; the most frequent cause is that ivory really should be kept under glass, in a cabinet if possible. The worst thing for it is to place it on a shelf over a fireplace, where fumes or smoke from any sort of fuel can reach it. It is also wise to guard against drafts, as sometimes a sudden change of temperature may crack it."

Ivory can be cleaned easily with soft water containing a few drops of ammonia and a little liquid detergent (not more than one percent of either) applied with a sponge. If the ivory is intricately carved, it may be necessary to use an artist's brush. On very thin ivory, such as carved flower petals, butterflies, and other similar delicate work, equal parts of water and alcohol can be used as a cleaning solution.

Before using any liquid cleaner on ivory, make sure that the sculptor has not used india ink to heighten any parts of the carving, such as the pupils of the eyes. If he has, use a dry cleaner, such as fine crumbs of soft india rubber massaged over the ivory to collect the surface dirt. Alter-

natively, ivory can be cleaned without using moisture by mixing whiting or precipitated chalk with alcohol to a thick cream, painting it on, allowing it to dry, and then brushing it lightly away.

Although it has been suggested that a safe way to bleach ivory is to saturate a wad of cotton wool with dilute hydrogen peroxide and keep this in contact with the ivory, I feel myself that if bleaching is necessary, it can be done much more safely by exposing the ivory to sunlight under a glass shade.

There are some difficulties in the way of the ordinary person learning how to criticize and appreciate ivory carvings. Of course most people like them, instinctively, especially if they can touch them and handle them, because ivory is one of the few substances that are delightful to handle. Because ivory forms an important part of the body (teeth), it feels natural and "right." To like something is not necessarily to appreciate it intelligently. Kineton Parkes once remarked that anyone could criticize or appreciate a drawing, because everyone could use a pencil. The same thing held true of paintings; most of us have used a paintbox at school. When it came to sculpture, though, that was a different affair. Criticism should be left to those who have actually held a graver. Most people do not even know the names of a sculptor's tools, much less know how to use them, and ivory carving is a very specialized art. Obviously the best way of being able to criticize and appreciate ivories is to learn how to carve them. I should not like to discourage anyone from doing this, but for those of us who prefer our experiences at second hand, here are a few selected comments from sculptors about the attraction of ivory for their public— most of what they have to say will be more immediately applicable to their patrons, because this is the only part of the public that a sculptor usually meets. Only very rarely do people write you to say that they liked your work, as they might to an author about his book.

"Ivory is a lovely material in color and texture," Jeanne Bell told me, "and I suppose anyone interested in small sculpture appreciates that, as well as the design." Gwynneth Holt said: "I don't really know why people buy ivories. I suppose they like the material itself, which is so beautiful, but the subject, and the way it is treated, is equally important. . . . Whatever the material—stone, wood, clay, or ivory—one gets to know and understand it and its limitations, and a design should be made to fit it. I usually buy things because I like them, and they appeal to me, and give pleasure."

Just as people who buy sporting pictures—especially pictures of horses—are supposed to be much more interested in horses, for example, than art, there is a strong suggestion that many patrons are more interested in the beautiful properties of ivory itself than in sculpture *per se*. Jeanne Bell comments: "I think most of my purchasers are people who like to make a small collection of ivories, and are not so much interested in other forms of sculpture. The hoped-for client with both money and artistic appreciation is rather a problem in these times."

A good ivory carving ought, first of all, to be made of ivory, a point many unwary purchasers overlook every year. It is quite easy to determine what really is ivory and what is merely imitation, and I have given a number of tests for doing so elsewhere.[1] A carving ought to have style, it should reflect the personality of the sculptor who made it, and should preferably be unmistakable as that person's work and his alone. (As has been already noticed, masters in sculpture tend to exert a strong influence over their followers. Everatt Gray always had by him an album of carefully collected photographs of Richard Garbe's work.) A good ivory should also have period. It should be referable to the era when it was made. Ivory carving is a timeless art, however, and no ivory carver would be particularly displeased if you told him his work reminded you of Romanesque or even Assyrian ivories. An ivory carving should be well designed and also well worked, prefer-

ably so that some of the tools used by the sculptor appear in his handiwork. Color is unimportant. "All colors are nice colors" Gwynneth Holt once remarked. So too is the kind of ivory used, with some reservations. Some ivories are much more homogeneous than others; mammoth ivory will show lots of cracks, walrus ivory has a gaping cavity at the bottom, while hippopotamus ivory sometimes shows little yellow cracks, depending on which teeth are used. Get to know your ivories and then you will know what to expect. Polish is also unimportant.

Sooner or later a collector will be offered an ivory that, though desirable in itself, needs repair. This is more likely through casual purchase from a fellow collector than from an antique shop, because shop owners and dealers well know the value of presenting ivories to customers in the best possible condition. If they have any broken ivories, they will wait till they get them repaired. These repairs are always done by an ivory carver. They are never a simple filling in of the broken parts with white plastic, a type of repair that is, regrettably, almost invariably seen in broken ivories in museums. The whole purpose of an ivory carving is that all the surfaces shall reflect light on every part of the work. If a gap is filled with plastic instead of ivory, this object is not achieved; it is as if a painting by an Old Master had been restored with dabs of white paint here and there. Instead, the missing sections are artistically recarved in the spirit of the whole piece and an invisible join is made. Jeanne Bell's experiences are of interest here: "I did quite a lot of ivory repairing two or three years ago. Mostly I had to replace very small hands and feet that had been broken off, or lost, in transit. So I carved a number of these, and sometimes pieces of costume, and fastened them on to the figures with small dowels of ivory, or in some cases, of wire. Holes for these dowels had to be drilled, of course, which was very tricky in the case of very small pieces. I have several times repaired very elaborate Japanese and Chinese pieces of carving, which are made in several pieces, very skillfully fixed together

---

1. Carson I. A. Ritchie, *Ivory Carving*, Arthur Barker, London, 1969.

"The Wild Ass" and "Ants," from "Animals of
the Bible," by the author.

with dowels of ivory."

There can be no harm in a sculptor-carved repair in ivory. For one thing, an honest dealer (I have never met any of the other kind) will hasten to point out to a customer that a repair has been made. For another, a piece of fresh ivory that has been inserted or added to an old carving can be detected by inspection under a quartz lamp. I would not myself like to subscribe to the dictum that fresh ivory always fluoresces yellow, and old ivory purple. I would like to know a little more about the kind of ivory from which a piece was made before I applied this test, because all ivories fluoresce rather differently. The join is quite obvious however.

A good ivory carver can carve in any style, and most ivory sculptors are very obliging about repairing breakages. Shortly before I arrived at Gwynneth Holt's studio, a distraught couple came to her door carrying a Chinese statue of a fisherman, whose rod had broken. Miss Holt left the very important commission on which she was working, picked up a boar's tusk, which was exactly the right curve for the fishing rod, and re-equipped the little fisherman. The collectors went away delighted, saying that the repair was better than the original.

It is not always easy to get in touch with ivory carvers. Ivory dealers see comparatively few of them because, as I have already said, sculptors use very little ivory. If you enquire for the nearest commercial ivory worker, the man who makes piano keys or hairbrush backs, he can sometimes help you. People who restore firearms usually have to do a lot of repairs in ivory and may be prepared to undertake repairs to carvings. If you put the repair through a dealer, he will of course expect a commission.

There is a lot to be said for collectors effecting their own repairs: they will save money, which should of course be spent buying new and exciting pieces; and they will learn a lot both about ivory and how carvings are put together. Elsewhere[2] I have given suggestions as to how the complete amateur can begin to carve ivory, and also how repairs can be made.

---

2. Carson I. A. Ritchie, *Ivory Carving*, London, 1969.

Index